ENDORSEMENTS FOR
THE CHURCH AND NEW MEDIA

Archbishop Timothy M. Dolan, archbishop of New York
"My expectation is that this book will give the Church courage and wisdom to embrace New Media as one of the premier gifts of God to evangelists of our day."

Cardinal Seán O'Malley, O.F.M. Cap., archbishop of Boston
"This book demonstrates how New Media is already impacting the Church and outlines many practical steps for dioceses, parishes, and individual Catholics to embrace it more broadly…. Everyone involved in communications and evangelization ministries for the Church should read it."

Cardinal Donald Wuerl, archbishop of Washington
"From the quill to the printing press to the modern app, the Church has faced the challenge of preaching the Word of God in a way that each generation will hear it. *The Church and New Media* offers an insightful contribution to the way in which the Church passes on the Gospel message in the age of new social communication. This book helps us understand both the potential and the challenges of blogging, tweeting, and all the multiple forms of the new communications. I am pleased to recommend this very useful guide for individuals, parishes, and diocesan workers who seek to use the New Media to proclaim the Gospel and pass on the faith."

Archbishop Charles Chaput, O.F.M. Cap., archbishop of Denver
"*The Church and New Media* is the best kind of reading: timely, vivid, and rich in valuable information. For anyone seeking to understand and use today's new technologies in advancing the Catholic faith, this book is an unsurpassed resource."

Monsignor Paul Tighe, secretary of the Vatican's Pontifical Council for Social Communications

"Brandon Vogt's book *The Church and New Media* is a wonderful guide to the emerging presence of American Catholic voices in the digital arena. The book is not primarily an instruction manual telling us how to use New Media; more significantly, it shows us what can be done. By showcasing some proven initiatives, it invites us to reflect on how we can witness to our faith in the new 'public square' that is being created by social media. We can learn from the expertise of those who are already actively ensuring that the Church is present in this 'new continent,' but perhaps more importantly, we can take heart from their enthusiasm and be encouraged by the fruitfulness of their labor."

Mike Aquilina, author and executive vice president of the St. Paul Center for Biblical Theology

"If St. Peter, St. Ignatius, and St. Augustine had access to today's New Media, they would do exactly the same things as the contributors to this book. *The Church and New Media* carries the Church's mission into the digital age and is better than a graduate degree in media. You'll learn 'what works' from Catholics who are already spreading the Gospel through these tools. Marshall McLuhan would be well pleased."

James Martin, S.J., author of *The Jesuit Guide to (Almost) Everything*

"This important new book reminds all Catholics of the need to use any means at our disposal to spread the Gospel. After all, Jesus of Nazareth used easy-to-understand images like birds, seeds, and clouds in the medium known as the parable to convey his message. Today's evangelical media are blogs, websites, and social media (and no doubt something invented in the last few months). If Jesus could speak about the birds of the air, then we should not be afraid of tweeting."

Amy Welborn, popular Catholic author and blogger

"In *The Church and the New Media*, Brandon Vogt presents helpful essays from a variety of Catholics active in online ministry. The experiences and advice of this diverse group of bloggers, social networkers, and Internet evangelists will be helpful to any Catholic seeking to utilize the Internet to present the Catholic faith, as well as to understand its risks and potential."

Elizabeth Scalia, managing editor of the *Catholic Portal* at Patheos.com and the blogger known as "The Anchoress"

"As the Catholic Church makes a dynamic entry into the virtual arena — encouraging its priests, religious, and laypeople to embrace alternative media, and introducing its own multi-media brand in News.va — *The Church and New Media* is that rarest of things: precisely the right book, released at precisely the right time. Brandon Vogt has a true journalist's ability to bring disparate components together for analysis and breakdown; here he manages to use well-known and newer voices to demonstrate the power of this revolutionary means of evangelization, and its lasting impact. This is relevant, timely reading for Catholics who wonder how emerging media can positively impact the life of faith in the 21st Century."

Sister Helena Burns, media literacy educator for the Daughters of St. Paul and Pauline Books and Media

"*The Church and New Media* is *the book* for all engaged Catholics to be reading and talking about! It is full of sage advice for utilizing the exciting panoply of New Media.

"Its unique format lets the Catholic New Media movers, shakers, and early-adopters tell their own stories. The book introduces us to some of its stellar leaders who are answering the call of both Pope John Paul II and Pope Benedict XVI to carry out the New Evangelization."

Mark Hart, vice president of Life Teen International and author of *Blessed Are the Bored in Spirit: A Young Catholic's Search for Meaning*

"*The Church and New Media* is a timely and necessary read for all serving the Church today. The book's lucid insights and practical ideas should be shared and replicated by Catholics around the globe.

"For years, the Church has been challenged to share the Gospel with a screen-based culture. But *The Church and New Media* offers some viable solutions, a sorely needed guide for the Church today.

"If those entrusted with handing on the faith subscribe to the principles within this book, the Gospel will undoubtedly take root in our modern, tech-savvy culture."

Dan Andriacco, communications director for the Archdiocese of Cincinnati and author of *Screen Saved*

"Brandon Vogt has compiled an outstanding handbook of digital evangelism, written by some of the most successful pioneers in the field. From theological underpinnings to practical advice, this book has something new to tell you wherever you are — from Catholic mom with a blogging itch to diocesan professional. I particularly appreciated the often-repeated admonition to avoid negativity in our digital communications and instead embrace the faith with joy. That's the way to evangelize!"

John Dyer, author of *From the Garden to the City: The Redeeming and Corrupting Power of Technology*

"Brandon Vogt has assembled some of the best examples of Catholics stepping into our media-saturated, technology-dominated world in order to draw people to Christ. Vogt is careful to point out the potential negatives that can come with today's technology, but rather than concluding that we should fearfully reject the new tools, he and his fellow writers show us how to enthusiastically and deftly embrace them."

THE CHURCH AND NEW MEDIA

BLOGGING CONVERTS,
ONLINE ACTIVISTS,
AND BISHOPS
WHO TWEET

BRANDON
VOGT

Our Sunday Visitor Publishing Division
Our Sunday Visitor, Inc.
Huntington, Indiana 46750

Contents

(Parts, Chapters, and Sidebars)

Foreword
Cardinal Seán O'Malley, O.F.M. Cap.

In July 2008, I accompanied a large group from the Archdiocese of Boston to Sydney, Australia, for World Youth Day. The whole experience of being with the Holy Father, many of my brother bishops and priests, and young people from throughout the globe was uplifting for all of us. Having attended many previous World Youth Day pilgrimages, I had expected the joy, hope, and love for the Church. But something happened on World Youth Day 2008 that made it a different and memorable experience for me, and one that told me that the Church had now entered a different era of evangelization.

This was the first World Youth Day since I had launched **Cardinal Seán's Blog** (CardinalSeansBlog.org) in September 2006. Young people from every continent introduced themselves and informed me that they regularly read my blog. Several commented about specific blog posts that they enjoyed, and we discussed them. This experience confirmed for me my belief in the immense reach of New Media vehicles — such as a blog — and also how effective these vehicles could be as tools of evangelization, particularly to young Catholics who have grown up with these technologies.

As the Holy Father and many others have written, New Media has created a fundamental shift in communication patterns comparable to the introduction of the printing press several centuries ago and has similarly instituted a new culture of communication. It is not just important but vital that the Church bring the Good News of Jesus Christ into that culture and infuse the "digital continent" with the leaven of our Catholic faith.

We are all called to be missionaries and evangelizers in our families, communities, workplaces, and social networks. Just as we expect great missionary orders to learn the culture of the natives they are evangelizing, we must also learn, live, and embrace the life and culture of the digital continent.

Effective use of social media can bring our Catholic community closer together as we live our great faith and carry on the mission Christ has entrusted to us. Bishop Ronald Herzog of Alexandria, Louisiana, led all the U.S. bishops in a discussion about New Media at the Fall General Assembly in November 2010. He started by proving that New Media is a powerful force, not a fad. Many people today, especially the young, turn first to New Media for information. Therefore, he explained that it would be disastrous if the Church didn't take it seriously and begin effectively utilizing these tools now to augment our existing communications media. The Church doesn't have to change its teachings to reach young people, but it must deliver the faith to them in a different way to reach them and be present.

This book, *The Church and New Media*, demonstrates how New Media is already impacting the Church and outlines many practical steps for dioceses, parishes, and individual Catholics to embrace it more broadly. Brandon Vogt, Our Sunday Visitor, and the trailblazing New Media pioneers that write each of the chapters have done a great service to the Church by sharing their experience and ideas. Everyone involved in communications and evangelization ministries for the Church should read it.

It was especially uplifting to read Jennifer Fulwiler's account in Chapter 2 of how Catholic blogs helped lead her from atheism to the Truth of the Catholic faith through the information and friendships she found as a young mother online. Let us pray that many other "Jennifer Fulwilers" will be led to experience the saving love of Jesus Christ through the Church's embracing and living on this digital continent.

The recommendations and best practices shared by the book's contributors assemble many years worth of wisdom for dioceses, parishes, and individual Catholics who are beginning their ministry on the digital continent, as well as those that want to strengthen their existing presence. I am confident that you will find the ideas shared in *The Church and New Media* helpful, whether you are a New Media novice or expert. Thank you for everything you have done, and everything you will do, to bring the Light of Christ and the warm welcome of our Catholic family to this new frontier.

God bless you.

✠ Cardinal Seán O'Malley, O.F.M. Cap.

Archbishop of Boston

// The Digital Continent //
Brandon Vogt

The Church and Old Media

Christianity reveals a God who uses all sorts of media to get his message across, from pillars of fire to bright stars, from burning bushes to a talking donkey. He delivered the Ten Commandments on chiseled rock, painted rainbows to signal his covenant, and used a cross to display his love.

However, the Bible doesn't mention God using emails, blog posts, podcasts, or e-books — and when the prophet Habakkuk [2:2] quotes God saying, "Write the vision; make it plain upon tablets," he wasn't promoting iPads, either! Even though these technologies don't show up in Scripture, history has shown that God showers down new mediums at specific times to spread his Word in new ways.

For its first one-and-a-half thousand years, Christianity's dominant form of communication was hand-copied print, with parchments, scrolls, and books transmitting sacred writings. These texts were used in the liturgy and were proclaimed at special religious gatherings. During these early centuries, if Christians wanted to absorb pieces of Scripture, they typically had to find a community that would read them aloud.

The 15th century, however, saw Christianity's first major communication shift. When Johannes Gutenberg invented the movable-type printing press, he influenced not only *what* Christians communicated but *how*. Through Gutenberg's invention, religious texts were quickly produced, copied, and disseminated across the world. This shifted the focus of Christianity from listening to reading, from the community to the individual, and from concrete images to abstract theology.

Roughly 450 years after this radical change, a new technology called "radio" entered the scene. The Catholic Church was one of the first to harness this new medium, with the charismatic Fulton Sheen beginning his weekly *Catholic Hour* in 1930.[1] The show's audience grew quickly, and after two decades, four million people tuned in each week to hear America's most famous evangelist.

In 1951, Sheen was appointed auxiliary bishop of New York and soon moved — along with the Church — to the world's next new technology: television. Sheen's *Life is Worth Living* show continued his radio success, attracting 30 million weekly viewers at its peak.[2]

Sheen wasn't alone as a prominent Catholic television personality. In 1981, Mother Angelica debuted EWTN, the Eternal Word Television Network. The network's early programming was broadcast from a garage at Our Lady of the Angels Monastery in Alabama. Today, EWTN is the largest religious media network in the world, reaching more than 146 million homes in 127 countries.[3]

Throughout history, the Church aptly discerned the power of each of these past technologies — print, radio, and television — even in light of each medium's disadvantages. But while the Church recognized the potency of these prior tools, nobody could have foreseen the power of what came next.

The Digital Revolution

In 1943, the president of IBM purportedly claimed that "there is a world market for maybe five computers." A few decades later, the president of another technology company asserted, "There is no reason anyone would want a computer in their home."[4]

In hindsight, neither man could have been more wrong. The last few decades have witnessed a digital explosion unimaginable 50 years ago, sparked by the advent of the Internet and its World Wide Web.

As in earlier times, the Church was quick to adopt these new tools. The Vatican created one of the Internet's earliest sites in 1995, making many Church documents available on the Web. The Vatican webpage modeled the style of most other pages over the next half-decade: static, information repositories featuring one-way communication — from the website to the user.

But a second wave of innovation began with the new millennium. The early 21st century introduced the burgeoning New Media, encompassing blogs, social media, text messaging, and other digital tools.

Though the classification is nebulous, New Media has many typical features that distinguish it from its predecessors. New Media usually provides on-demand access to content anytime, anywhere, on any digital device,[5] accomplishing this through the vast interconnectivity of the Web.

But a primary, defining characteristic of all New Media is *dialogue*. While traditional media features static content and one-way flows of information — like the Vatican's early website — New Media transmits content through connection and conversation. It enables people around the world to share, comment on, and discuss a wide variety of topics. Unlike any of the past technologies, New Media is grounded on interactive community.

One of the first examples of New Media emerged around the turn of the millennium. Blogs — short for "web logs" — were introduced as websites featuring regularly updated entries. In contrast to traditional sites, blogs allowed readers to interact with the original author, forming the social backbone of the digital revolution.

Blogs helped spark the first social network, Friendster, which debuted in 2002. Friendster gathered real-world friends into an online community and became popular fast: in its first three months, the site gained three million users. Friendster was followed a year later by MySpace, which competed with Friendster but sported a more youth-friendly culture.

In 2004, a new social networking site was launched by students at Harvard University as a way to connect U.S. college students.[6] Facebook, as it was eventually branded, had an appealing exclusivity — you had to have a college email address to join. This made it especially popular among young adults, who didn't want to mingle online with parents or children. The site gained over 200 million users in its first eight months, eventually opening itself up to the world.[7]

YouTube was the next major New Media creation. Produced in 2005 and now owned by search-engine giant Google, YouTube is the most popular online video destination. The site receives over two billion views per day, nearly double the prime-time audience of all three major television networks combined.[8]

One year after YouTube, the micro-blogging service Twitter was introduced, inviting users to share "tweets" of 140 characters or less. The site now has over 190 million users who generate 65 million new tweets each day.[9]

The statistics surrounding these and other New Media tools simply boggle the mind:

- The average American spends 66 hours per month on a computer outside of work.[10] While pornography had once been the dominant Internet activity, social media has now taken the top slot.[11]

- Facebook, the Internet's most popular website,[12] has over 500 million users, half of whom log in every single day. If Facebook were a country, it would be the world's third largest, behind only China and India.[13] Facebook users spend over 700 billion minutes each month on the site, sharing over 30 billion pieces of content.[14]

- YouTube visitors watch over two billion videos every day. Every minute, 24 hours of new video are uploaded to the site.[15]

- Singers Lady Gaga, Justin Bieber, and Britney Spears each have over 6.5 million Twitter followers.[16] Any message they "tweet" will instantly reach millions of people in a matter of seconds.

- The Internet features over 200 million blogs, according to conservative estimates.[17] More than 75 percent of Internet users regularly read blogs.[18]

- Almost half of Americans have listened to a podcast, while two-thirds of those people have listened in their car.[19]

- Seventy-two percent of Americans — including 87 percent of teens — communicate through text messaging.[20] Last year alone, Americans sent 1.8 trillion text messages.[21]

Existing in a world that has dramatically embraced New Media, the Church finds herself at a crossroads. This is the new habitat for the majority of Christians.

The question is, will the Church take up residence too?

The Digital Continent

At the 43rd World Communications Day, Pope Benedict XVI encouraged Catholics to boldly enter the "digital continent." Despite being over 80 years old, Benedict keenly recognizes this digital world for what it is: a ripe mission field for the Church.

Many individuals have already staked claim to chunks of this online land, establishing rich hubs of evangelization and formation. Others have built welcoming communities that are expanding every day. And some have harnessed the power of New Media to serve the common good.

Throughout this book, you'll find contributions and highlights from many New Media pioneers, guides who are navigating the Church through uncharted digital waters. The book is divided into four sections, each emphasizing one of the Church's main online missions.

The first section covers New Media and evangelization. Father Robert Barron explains how he uses New Media to engage the secular online world — including its "new atheists" — while answering what he deems the "YouTube heresies." Jennifer Fulwiler recounts how she blogged her way from atheism to Catholicism. And Marcel LeJeune, a college campus minister at Texas A&M University, describes how New Media connects young adults to the Church.

In the second section, which covers New Media and formation, you'll learn how these tools can form and strengthen one's faith. Mark Shea explores the beauties and dangers of Christian blogging, while Taylor Marshall discusses how New Media can unwrap ancient truths. Father Dwight Longenecker then describes how he uses his blog to dialogue with people from other Christian traditions.

The book's third section concerns New Media and community. Scot Landry and Matt Warner offer a wealth of practical tips on how dioceses and parishes can implement New Media tools. And Lisa Hendey explores the growing online community fostered by New Media's social nature.

The final section covers New Media and the common good. In his chapter, Thomas Peters rallies Christians to be faithful online activists. And Shawn Carney tells the story of how the world's largest pro-life movement used New Media to save lives and change hearts.

In addition to each of these chapters, dozens of sidebars appear throughout the book. Some feature excerpts from Church documents relevant to New Media, while others highlight Catholics who are using New Media creatively and effectively.

Throughout the book, you'll discover many unique vantage points on the Church and New Media relationship, from young to old, clergy to laypeople, and men to women. Since this digital revolution spans all demographics and all spheres of the Church, this book approaches it from many different angles.

One final note: New Media can at times be intimidating. But the learning curve isn't steep, and you're not alone.

To help you out as you journey across the digital continent, I've included a Glossary in the back of the book, which defines some common New Media terms. In addition, the book's Appendix provides many New Media recommendations, while the book's website (www.ChurchAndNewMedia.com) includes even more helpful content.

Giving the Internet a Soul

The Church can't change her responses to Gutenberg's printing press, the radio, or the television; they are forever fixed in history. But at the onset of this digital revolution, her response to New Media is wide open.

The world is waiting and listening in the virtual sphere. Will the Church remain silent, or will her voice be proclaimed from the rooftops (and the laptops)? Will she plunge the message of Christ into Facebook feeds, blog posts, podcasts, and text messages, or will she be digitally impotent?

If the Church's promotion of evangelization, formation, community, and the common good is to continue throughout future generations, she must harness these technologies and utilize them well.

In this book, you'll witness the Church's first steps across the digital continent. And by the end, you'll be compelled to join the march yourself.

May this guide stir your imagination and excitement as you help give the Internet a soul!

> *"Without fear we must set sail on the digital sea, facing into the deep with the same passion that has governed the ship of the Church for two thousand years…. [W]e want to qualify ourselves by living in the digital world with a believer's heart, helping to give a soul to the Internet's incessant flow of communication."[22]*
>
> — POPE BENEDICT XVI (2010)

// Part One //

Put Out Into the Deep: New Media and Evangelization

CHAPTER 1
// The Virtual Areopagus: Digital Dialogue With the Unchurched //
Father Robert Barron

Two Self-Inflicted Wounds

Even the most cursory glance at the statistics reveals that the Church in the United States is in a perilous condition. A 2008 Pew Forum study revealed that the fastest-growing religious group in America is the "nones," that is to say, those who have no official religious affiliation.[23] Currently, one in six Americans are not affiliated with any religious organization. And 25 percent of cradle Catholics have left their childhood faith. In fact, many studies have confirmed that the second-largest "religious" denomination in America is ex-Catholics. A Pew statistic that I found particularly telling is that 27 percent of Americans do not expect to have a religious funeral — a state of affairs unimaginable 50 years ago. More to it, numbers in regard to attendance at Mass are not encouraging: somewhere between 20 and 30 percent of Catholics attend the liturgy on a regular basis. And if one were to remove immigrants from that count — Filipinos, Vietnamese, and especially Hispanics — the numbers would sink to European lows.

Further, numerous studies have indicated that there is very little discernible difference in general behavior and attitude between Christians and secularists. Christians don't display a distinctive profile over and against the general culture; instead, they demonstrate the same allegiance to money, sex, and personal fulfillment as anyone else. And their views on central moral issues, from war and peace to birth control and abortion more or less track with the general population. Now, there are multiple causes for this decline, and in the context of this brief chapter I could never begin to explore them with even relative adequacy. But I would like to draw attention to two causes that I believe are especially important. Both are self-inflicted wounds from which the whole body of Christ continues to suffer.

The first is the clergy sex-abuse scandal. Through the wicked acts of a small percentage of priests and a small percentage of bishops who refused to deal with the problem, the Church has been massively wounded, and this wound is still open, still festering and infecting the rest of the body of Christ. Our attempts to preach, teach, and evangelize — both within the Church and without — are hugely compromised by this terrible fact. Though necessary and welcome institutional reforms have been made, the wound has not healed, not by a long shot. Fairly or not, official representatives of the Church are seen by many as corrupt, dissembling, clueless, and indifferent. If Aristotle is right in saying that the "ethos" of the speaker is the most important element in the act of persuasion, we shouldn't be surprised that people don't find us persuasive.

The second self-inflicted wound has affected, above all, the mind of the Church. Vatican II was, of course, informed by a formidable theological intelligence, and its purpose, ultimately, was missionary. It wanted to present the age-old faith to the modern world in a compelling way. But, as innumerable commentators have pointed out, the reception of Vatican II was, to say the least, problematic. In the United States at any rate, the missionary impulse to transform the culture devolved into a program of cultural accommodation. As a famous slogan of the time had it, "The world sets the agenda for the Church."

The concern of those who formed my generation (I went to first grade in 1965) was to make Catholicism appealing to the culture, and they therefore softened the edges of the faith, producing what I've termed a "beige Catholicism." There was an uncertain, hand-wringing quality to the Catholicism of my youth, because our intellectual leaders had lost confidence in the great Catholic story and tried, over and again, to translate it into terms acceptable to modernity. And this usually meant a translation into moral and psychological categories. The end result was that our preaching and teaching seemed, more often than not, a faint echo of what the culture was already saying.

Relatedly, apologetics got a very bad name during this period. Defending or explaining the faith to a presumably hostile or skeptical audience was seen as retrograde, defensive, pre-conciliar. We looked, at every turn, for points of contact with other religions and with the secular culture. Certainly in the West, the culture has not come running into the arms of the Church. Instead — and this was to a degree a post-September 11th phenomenon — elements of the high culture turned on us with a good deal of hostility, and when it did so, we were largely defenseless, having abandoned our own intellectual and apologetic tradition. We had become largely inept at telling our distinctive story, and so the world found it exceptionally easy either to co-opt our story or to simply dismiss it out of hand.

In very recent years, we have witnessed the rise of a particularly aggressive "new" atheism, whose mark is deep hostility toward religion (especially Christianity), which it perceives as irrational and therefore as violent. But we are often toothless in the face of this attack — as becomes clear in the number of representatives of Christianity who are often easily outmaneuvered by Christopher Hitchens, Richard Dawkins, and company.

For the past 15 years, I've been engaged in the work of evangelizing the culture. I've written 10 books of theology and spirituality; I've taught courses in philosophy and systematic theology at Mundelein Seminary, one the largest seminaries in the United States; I've broadcast and podcasted over 500 sermons; I've lectured business and civic leaders; and I've published dozens of articles in learned and popular journals. But I believe that the most effective work I've done in this arena is through the Internet.

My ministry, Word on Fire, maintains an interactive website on which my writings and sermons are featured and on which are posted over 170 videos that I've done for YouTube, today's most popular online video site in the world. These are commentaries on books, movies, music, popular culture, high culture, and current events. When Word on Fire launched these videos three years ago, we did so in the attitude of explorers and experimenters. We really had no idea whether they would attract any attention at all on YouTube, which is the virtual Areopagus: the place where all ideas are debated. To our delight and surprise, they garnered an audience rather quickly, and as of today over 1.4 million people have watched the videos.

> *"The Internet causes billions of images to appear on millions of computer monitors around the planet. From this galaxy of sight and sound will the face of Christ emerge and the voice of Christ be heard? For it is only when his face is seen and his voice heard that the world will know the glad tidings of our redemption. This is the purpose of evangelization. And this is what will make the Internet a genuinely human space, for if there is no room for Christ, there is no room for man."[24]*
>
> — BLESSED JOHN PAUL II, MESSAGE FOR THE 36TH WORLD COMMUNICATIONS DAY (2002)
>
> *"Dear Brothers and Sisters, I ask you to introduce into the culture of this new environment of communications and information technology the values on which you have built your lives. In the early life of the Church, the great Apostles and their disciples brought the Good News of Jesus to the Greek and Roman world. Just as, at that time, a fruitful evangelization required that careful attention be given to understanding the culture and customs of those pagan peoples so that the truth of the gospel would touch their hearts and minds, so also today, the proclamation of Christ in the world of new technologies requires a profound knowledge of this world if the technologies are to serve our mission adequately."[25]*
>
> — POPE BENEDICT XVI, MESSAGE FOR THE 43RD WORLD COMMUNICATIONS DAY (2009)

When this outreach commenced, I had no idea that viewers could comment on the videos. I quickly discovered that they could. To date, over 40,000 comments have been posted, and I must confess that the vast majority of them are negative — which is not surprising, given the fact that the YouTube audience is largely unchurched and secularized. Many of these are young men — men in their 20s and 30s. Outside of New Media, what better way is there to engage a secular-minded, anti-ecclesial, 25-year-old male? These videos offer a prime way to reach this demographic.

Since I can respond to these postings, I have an opportunity I would have in no other way, namely, to engage people who would never dream of coming to any of the institutions of the Catholic Church. Though some of my interlocutors are simply thoughtless or obscene, many of them are sincere seekers who, perhaps to their great surprise, find themselves in dialogue with a priest in regard to some of the deepest questions.

These lively exchanges on the YouTube forums have enabled me to discern, clearly enough, some of the basic patterns of resistance to the faith, some of the typical blocks to the acceptance of the Christian story.

In his message for the 43rd World Communications Day, Pope Benedict XVI counseled that using New Media to spread the faith "requires a profound knowledge of this world if the technologies are to serve our mission adequately."[26] Before using these new tools, Catholics should understand the patterns of the world with which they are engaging.

Though I cannot claim that my findings here rise to the level of sociological science, I believe that they are fairly good indicators of what the skeptical, secularized world — especially that part of it under the age of 40 — is thinking.

I have identified the four patterns of resistance — the four "YouTube heresies," if you will — as deep confusion about the meaning of the word "God," deep confusion about the correct manner of interpreting the Bible, deep confusion about the relationship between religion and science, and finally, deep confusion about the rapport between religion and violence.

The Meaning of the Word "God"

In his *Seven Storey Mountain*, Thomas Merton recalled the first time he read Etienne Gilson's *The Spirit of Medieval Philosophy* and encountered a philosophically sophisticated understanding of God as *ipsum esse* (the sheer act of being itself). He was flabbergasted because he had assumed that God was, in his words, a "noisy and dramatic" mythological being.

Again and again, in my dialogues on YouTube, I encounter the characterization of God as "a sky fairy," an "invisible friend," or my favorite, "the flying spaghetti monster." This last one comes from the militant atheist Richard Dawkins, who insinuates that there is as much evidence for God as for this fantastic imaginary creature.

Almost no one with whom I dialogue considers the possibility that God is not one being among many, not the "biggest thing around," not something that can be categorized or defined in relation to other things. Throughout his career, Thomas Aquinas insisted that God is best described, not as *ens summum* (highest being), but rather as *ipsum esse* (the subsistent act of being itself). As such, God is not a thing or existent among many. In fact, Aquinas specifies, God cannot be placed in any genus, even the genus of being. This distinction — upon which so much of Christian theology hinges — is lost on almost everyone with whom I speak on YouTube.

One of the best indicators of this confusion is the repeated demand for "evidence" of God's existence, by which my interlocutors typically mean some kind of scientifically verifiable trace of this elusive and most likely mythological being. My attempts to tell them that the Creator of the entire universe cannot be, by definition, an object within the universe are met, usually, with complete incomprehension.

I am convinced that apologists for the faith must revive some of the classical arguments for God's existence, not simply to hold off the atheist counterclaim but also to demonstrate precisely what thoughtful Christians mean when they speak of God. When I was coming of age theologically, very little mind was paid to these proofs, for they were seen as unbiblical and philosophically unpersuasive, but both of those charges are, I believe, unjustified. Rightly formulated, they open the mind of any objective inquirer to the Creator God to whom the Bible consistently bears witness.

I have found that the argument from contingency is particularly effective. It runs roughly as follows. We humans are contingent beings in the measure that we had parents, that we eat and drink, and that we breathe. But those elements upon which we depend for our existence — parents, food and drink, oxygen — are themselves conditioned, caused, contingent. We cannot go on endlessly appealing to similarly conditioned things, and therefore we must come, inevitably, to some reality which exists, not dependently but unconditionally, through the power of its own essence.

This demonstration has the great virtue of being a pithy and clear proof of precisely the God who is *ipsum esse* and therefore the ground and creator of all finite being. Some of my interlocutors, influenced by the popular pantheism so rampant today, concede that there might be a noncontingent ground of contingency, but they identify it simply with matter or energy. Here the Big Bang theory is quite helpful, since it indicates how time and matter themselves are radically contingent and hence in need of further causal explanation.

Word on Fire

When it comes to spreading the Gospel, few groups use New Media better than **Word on Fire** (www.WordOnFire.org), a global media ministry based out of Chicago. Word on Fire has a simple but revolutionary goal: to evangelize the culture. Led by renowned theologian Father Robert Barron, the ministry spreads the Gospel through its blog, an interactive website, YouTube videos, Facebook pages, and a podcast featuring over 500 homilies from Father Barron.

The Word on Fire team fully recognizes the necessity of entering the digital arena. Assistant director Father Steve Grunow explains, "If the Church does not authentically and boldly present itself in the context of the New Media, others will present the Church, and many of these presentations will be erroneous or hostile."

Through their New Media engagement, the Word on Fire website draws in over 100,000 people a month, and to date their YouTube videos have been viewed over 1.4 million times. The videos, in particular, have attracted numerous people who would otherwise never engage a priest or set foot in a church.

Word on Fire's success in New Media evangelization has led many to compare Father Barron to the 20th century's great media evangelist, Archbishop Fulton Sheen.[27] Like Archbishop Sheen, Father Barron's ministry engages culture on its own terrain, meeting people through anonymous media outlets in the comfort of their own homes.

Whether through video commentaries on popular movies or blog reviews of best-selling atheistic literature, the Word on Fire team uses new technologies to gaze on culture through a Christian lens.

"Engaging New Media is the modern equivalent of 'going and telling it on the mountain,' " explains Rozann Carter, production assistant at Word on Fire. "If our faith defines who we are and becomes part of our every expression, it should move through our keyboards and illuminate our computer screens."

Biblical Interpretation

The second "heresy" has to do with the reading of the Bible. To state it bluntly, most of my conversation partners on YouTube think that Catholics approach the Bible the way Muslims approach the Koran, namely, as a text that was directly dictated by God; and they therefore conclude that the Scriptures should be interpreted in a straightforward, unequivocal manner. I have discovered, in a word, that biblical literalism is by no means restricted to the fundamentalist camp. The comedian Bill Maher's film *Religulous* (my commentary on which has received 130,000 visits and over 7,500 comments) is especially instructive in this regard. Maher spends much of the movie interrogating pretty simple people concerning the Genesis account of Adam and Eve and the story of Jonah and the whale, wondering how anyone in the 21st century could possibly believe such nonsense.

One of the most basic clarifications I make is that the Bible is not so much a *book* as a *library*, which is to say, a collection of texts from a variety of literary genres. The opening chapters of Genesis are religious saga; the Song of Songs is a love poem; 1 Samuel and 2 Samuel are theologically informed history; Paul to the Romans is a letter; Daniel is an apocalypse, etc. But most of my critics want to approach each of these texts with the same set of interpretive lenses, namely, that which is appropriate to the reading of newspapers or strictly historical texts.

A good deal of the problem flows from the faulty understanding of God I outlined above. If God is construed as one being among many, then his causal efficacy competes with ours. In regard to Scripture, this means that the Bible is his book, not ours. But the Catholic sense, of course, is that the Bible is, as Vatican II puts it in *Dei Verbum* (n. 13), "the words of God, expressed in human language."[28] Given God's unique metaphysical makeup, it is altogether possible to speak of a divine authorship that does not compete with or preclude real human authorship. But to admit human authorship means to admit cultural conditioning, historical context, the particularity of literary genre, authorial intention, etc. In a word, it is to admit the need for interpretation.

A difficulty I face again and again is that apparently an entire generation has been raised with very little feel for literature or poetry, for the manner in which literary texts mean. There is a marked tendency among my interlocutors to see truth as identical to fact or journalistic reportage. When I observe that certain biblical texts are metaphorical, poetic, or symbolic in nature, I am invariably accused of "cherry-picking," conveniently isolating those parts of the Bible that tell what "really happened" from those that don't. I counter that nonliteral texts such as Virgil's *Aeneid*, Dante's *Divine Comedy*, Eliot's *The Wasteland*, Swift's *Gulliver's Travels*, and Melville's *Moby Dick* are bearers of profound truth indeed, though they convey their truth in a distinctively nonscientific or nonhistorical way.

Perhaps this resistance to more sophisticated readings of the Bible shouldn't surprise us, given the dominance of fundamentalism in the American media. Those who have seized and used the mass media most effectively have been evangelical Protestants, and thus their version of Christianity and biblical interpretation is the best known. I have found that the Catholic approach to the Scriptures, which involves deep attention to genre and a keen interest in symbolic, spiritual, and allegorical styles of reading, is largely unknown.

Scientism

A third "heresy" I consistently encounter is scientism, by which I mean the reduction of knowledge to the scientific way of knowing. The roots of this problem go back to the dawn of the modern period, to the work of Descartes and Bacon. Those two massively influential figures urged European academics to turn their intellectual energy from theology and abstract metaphysics to the mastery of nature, which is to say, to engineering, medicine, and practical science. And these have certainly been the most followed marching orders in intellectual history. The sciences — and their attendant technologies — have been so massively successful that people have come, understandably enough, to see the scientific way of knowing as the only valid epistemological path.

Time and again, my conversation partners on YouTube urge me to admit that the only valid form of truth is that which comes as a result of the scientific method: observing the world, gathering evidence, marshalling arguments, performing experiments, etc. I customarily respond that the scientific method is effective indeed when investigating empirical phenomena but that it is useless when it comes to questions of a more philosophical nature, such as the determination of the morally right and wrong, the assessment of something's aesthetic value, or the settling of the question why there is something rather than nothing.

More to it, I argue that to hold consistently to scientism involves one in an operational contradiction, for the claim that all knowledge is reducible to scientific knowledge is not itself a claim that can be justified scientifically! But this appeal to metaphysics and philosophy strikes most of my conversation partners as obscure at best, obfuscating at worst.

A large part of the problem here is that we have lost, in the wider culture, the appreciation of philosophy as a mediating discipline between religion and science. We hold science to be rational, and thus we say that religion, which is clearly not science, must be irrational. A very good example of this problem is the recent statement of the physicist Stephen Hawking, perhaps the best-known scientist in the world, concerning the origins of the universe.

Presumably, on Hawking's reading, the universe can burp itself out of nothing, without any need for a Creator. The problem, of course, is that there is deep ambiguity and equivocation in regard to the word "nothing" as Hawking employs it. By it, he seems to mean a "fluctuating quantum vacuum" which has energy and even spatial extension. To refer to this rather substantial state of affairs as "nothing" is confounding indeed to the philosopher who uses "nothing" to designate absolute nonbeing.

Almost all of my interlocutors believe the 19th-century myth that the sciences emerged out of a terrible struggle against religion. The Galileo case, persistently reiterated, is the paradigm for understanding the rapport between religion and science. I remind them, with equal insistence, that the Galileo affair is one paragraph in one chapter of a much longer book. There was in fact, I argue, a deep congruence between religion and science in the minds of most of the great founders of the physical sciences, from Pascal and Descartes to Newton and Tycho Brahe. More to it, the instigator of modern genetics was a friar, and the formulator of the Big Bang theory of cosmic origins was a priest. Though well known to Catholic intellectuals, these facts, I find, are surprising revelations to most of my audience.

I make the case continually, furthermore, that the sciences emerged where and when they did precisely due to certain theological assumptions — corollaries of the doctrine of creation — namely, that the universe is not divine and that it is marked, in every detail, by intelligibility. If the universe were considered divine or sacred, one would never be inclined to experiment upon it or subject it to invasive rational analysis. The doctrine of creation from nothing involves just this implication that the world is radically other than God. Further, unless the universe was understood as fundamentally intelligible, no scientist could get his work under way.

The biologist, the chemist, the physicist, the psychologist, and the ophthalmologist must take for granted, on the basis of a mystical assumption, that the aspect of the world that they go out to meet is endowed with intelligible structure. But once again, it is the doctrine of creation —the teaching that all things are made through the divine Word — that undergirds this confident assumption. I appeal again and again to the inescapably theological foundations of the sciences in order to counterbalance the disproportionate weight given by almost all of my conversation partners to the Galileo paradigm.

Catholics Come Home

While "Catholic" still remains the most popular religious affiliation in America, the second-largest group is "former-Catholics." Roughly 25 percent of Americans are self-professing Catholics, while 10 percent of Americans have abandoned the title.[29]

At a time when evangelizing the formerly churched is just as vital as reaching the unchurched, **Catholics Come Home** (www.CatholicsComeHome.org) has made it their mission to reach those who have left the faith. The group carries out this mission through evocative television commercials that point former Catholics to the website.

Once on the site, visitors find much to explore. You can read through clear, reasonable explanations of Church teachings. You can watch videos of real stories and real people who have returned to the faith they previously drifted away from. And you can read a regularly updated blog featuring articles, book recommendations, and success stories from Catholics Come Home campaigns. All of the website and ad content has been carefully screened and edited by a renowned group of Catholic theologians, so it presents Catholicism both beautifully and accurately.

Catholics Come Home has had tremendous success in reigniting the faith of thousands of people around the world. In one survey, over 53 percent of inactive Catholics or former Catholics considered returning to or checking out the Catholic Church after viewing just one of the Catholics Come Home commercials.[30] So far, an estimated 200,000 people have returned to parishes in the United States as a result of the campaign.[31]

Many individual dioceses have experienced similar results. For example, in its Catholics Come Home media campaign, the Diocese of Phoenix saw an increase of 12 percent in Mass attendance throughout the diocese, despite a neutral population growth. Using a bilingual Catholics Come Home campaign, the Diocese of Corpus Christi, Texas, experienced a 17.7 percent increase in Mass attendance. Overall, the first dozen dioceses that participated in a campaign saw their average Mass attendance increase 10 percent.[32]

Through their efforts, Catholics Come Home exemplifies the "new evangelization" encouraged by recent popes, reviving the latent faith of many who have ignored it.

Religion and Violence

A fourth "heresy" has to do with religion and violence, and it is probably the most powerful and deep-seated that I confront. The events of September 11, 2001, stirred up the old Enlightenment-era argument that religion is invariably violent, precisely because it is irrational. It seems that since religious people cannot offer reasonable arguments for their positions, they finally have recourse only to force when they seek to propagate their faith or when they confront religious views alien to their own. I have found that the enemies of the faith are only too well acquainted with the examples of violence and misbehavior in the history of the Church: the Crusades, the Inquisition, the witch-hunts, the persecution of Jews, and to bring things up to date, the abuse of children by Catholic clergy.

Innumerable critics ask me how I could in good faith even represent an institution that is responsible for so much mayhem. Here I am compelled to make a distinction between the divine and human dimensions of the Church, between the mystical body of Christ and the deeply flawed human beings who belong to that body. In its sacraments (especially the Eucharist), its liturgy, its apostolic governance, its Scripture, its essential teachings, and in the lives of its saints, the Church is the font of living water, the spotless bride of Christ. But this holiness does not preclude the possibility of Church people, even of the highest rank, doing stupid, violent, and immoral things. I am also not hesitant in reminding my secularist critics that the worst violence in human history — that perpetrated by Hitler, Stalin, Mao, and Pol Pot in the last century — was the fruit, not of religion, but of fiercely secularist and anti-religious ideologies.

The second major area of concern under this rubric is the Bible Itself — more precisely, those passages that seem to indicate that God commands acts of terrible violence. Once again, my critics are only too prepared to cite chapter and verse. They draw attention especially to the Book of Joshua, which features a blitzkrieging invasion of the Promised Land and, it seems, a divinely sanctioned ethnic cleansing of the native peoples conquered by Israel. And they bring to light those passages in the Samuel cycle which involve, it appears, a divine command to place on enemy peoples "the ban" — which is to say, the slaughter of every man, woman, child, and animal. Indeed, my critics are quick to remind me that King Saul falls out of favor with the prophet Samuel and with God precisely because he (Saul) failed to carry out the divine edict to put the ban on the Amalekites. Not to put too fine a point on it, they wonder how I could worship or recommend to others such a wicked God.

The great tradition provides a number of interpretive helps in this regard, and we should explore them with some care. A first observation is that, for Christians, the entire Bible must be read from the standpoint of Jesus, crucified and risen from the dead. A passage from the Book of Revelation is particularly illuminating here. John the visionary is within the heavenly temple, and he spies a scroll sealed with seven seals and representing the whole of Scripture or even the whole of history. He weeps because no one comes forward to unseal the text. Finally, the announcement is made that the Lion of Judah, who has triumphed, can perform the task. Then John sees, not a lion or a Davidic warrior, but rather a Lamb that seemed to have been slain (Revelation 5:1-7).

The point is clear: the nonviolent and forgiving Christ, slain on the cross and risen from the dead, is the hermeneutical key to the entire Bible and to the whole of the human story. When Christians survey the Bible, therefore, they do so through the interpretive lens of Jesus the Lamb. Thus, any reading of Scripture running counter to that fundamental Logos ought to be regarded as an illegitimate interpretation. The God disclosed in Jesus of Nazareth simply cannot be coherently understood as a bloodthirsty advocate of blitzkrieg, arbitrary killing, and genocide.

How then ought we to approach the difficult texts that I cited above? We might, first, appreciate them as theological/poetic expressions of the power and authority of God. A warlike ancient people would rather naturally lean toward a metaphor of military conquest in order to express the irresistibility of God's power. And they would see the absolute nature of the victory as evocative of the absolute quality of the divine force. One might say, therefore, that these texts are a poetic version of the creedal declaration: "I believe in one God, the Father almighty."

Secondly, since the Bible is "the words of God, expressed in human language," we might be sensitive to the progressive nature of biblical revelation, a theme suggested by Irenaeus in the second century. God is slowly, gradually educating the human race in his ways, and this means that he adapts himself to varying and evolving human modes of understanding. We cannot, therefore, simply isolate one passage, one moment in the Bible and say, without further explanation, this is the final revelation of God.

A third perspective — and to my mind the most important — is that the violent passages of the Bible ought to be read as spiritual metaphors, tropes for the terrible struggle between the ways of God and the ways of sin. Origen long ago commented that, in many of the biblical stories, the Israelites should be appreciated as evocative of all that is congruent with the will of God and that the enemies of Israel — Amalekites, Egyptians, Assyrians, Babylonians, Greeks, and Romans — symbolize all that stands athwart the divine purposes. A strong indication within the Bible itself that Origen is on to something is the conclusion of the great story, in the Book of Exodus, of the Israelites' battle against the Amalekites: "The Lord will have war with Amalek from generation to generation" (Exodus 17:16). On the assumption that the tale from Exodus is simply a straightforward historical account of Israel's struggle against a petty ancient Middle Eastern tribe, that claim makes little sense.

And with this more metaphorical reading in mind, we can make much better sense of Saul's fall from grace. By refusing to put the ban on Amalek, Saul was playing games with evil, indeed using evil for his own purposes. Consider the manner in which we typically deal in half-measures with evil, toying with it, using it in fact to our advantage, when we should simply be eliminating it. I'm quite sure that a man's A.A. sponsor would be less than satisfied upon hearing that his charge was taking only one drink a week and that a wife would be anything but delighted to hear that her husband was faithful to her 90 percent of the time. Certain forms of evil are so repugnant to human flourishing that they simply have to be eliminated. The ban must be placed on them. Saul spared the Amalekite king Agag, but the prophet Samuel, as the Bible not so delicately puts it, "hewed Agag in pieces" (1 Samuel 15:33). Read in a purely literalistic way, this passage is brutal indeed; but read metaphorically and spiritually, its depths open up: sometimes hacking evil to pieces is the only proper measure.

Conclusion

I recently went to visit my niece, a senior in high school at the time, and noticed a stack of her schoolbooks. The top book on the pile was the great *Hamlet* — not the CliffNotes *Hamlet*, not *Hamlet* "for Dummies," but Shakespeare's *Hamlet*. Underneath that was Virgil's *Aeneid*, which she was reading in Latin. Below that was a thick physics textbook, bristling with complexity.

But underneath her physics book was a big paperback book with a nice, quaint picture on the cover. The pages were filled with large print and plenty of other pretty pictures. That text, simplistic and juvenile, was her book for religion.

For literature, she was reading classical works, some of them in their original languages. For science, she was reading complex physics material. But for religion, she was essentially assigned a comic book.

We have a smart tradition — the Catholic tradition is intellectually profound and rich. So when spreading the faith, especially through New Media, we can't afford to dumb it down if the world is to find our story compelling.

For this reason, the content that Catholics share through New Media is every bit as important as mastery of the mediums themselves. The "YouTube heresies" exhibit this point. When serious-minded secularists engage Catholicism, the Church can't afford to reply to them with comic-book responses. The most powerful digital witness is the one which reveals Catholicism in all of its richness, intelligence, and texture. When using New Media, we must not water down the faith.

Finally, I should like to return to an image which I invoked at the outset, namely, the Areopagus, the great Athenian public law court into which St. Paul intrepidly ventured. The Areopagus was a place where all of the rival philosophical and religious ideas of the period were advertised and publicly debated. Paul's announcement of the one true God who made the heavens and the earth, and who had been definitively revealed in the resurrection of Jesus from the dead, was met mostly with derision. And yet a few commented, "We will hear you again about this" (Acts 17:32).

I take great comfort in this passage, for, as I mentioned, I think of the Internet as a sort of virtual Areopagus, a "space" in which a practically infinite variety of philosophies, religions, points of view, and personal prejudices are on display. Like Paul, I have endeavored to enter that space with the message of Jesus, and also like Paul, I've been met with, for the most part, opposition and derision. However, there are those few — and I hear from them every day — who do indeed listen. And some of them even come to the fullness of faith, just as those few who had patience with Paul in Athens became the seeds of European Christianity.

It would be unwise in the extreme for the Church to absent itself from the virtual Areopagus for fear of rejection or contradiction. We should enter it with the courage, intelligence, and sheer panache of St. Paul.

Father Robert Barron is an acclaimed author, speaker, and theologian. He is America's first podcasting priest and one of the world's most innovative teachers of Catholicism. His global, nonprofit media ministry called **Word on Fire** (www. WordOnFire.org) reaches millions of people by utilizing advanced and emerging technologies to draw people into or back to the faith.

Father Barron is the Francis Cardinal George Professor of Faith and Culture at the University of St. Mary of the Lake/ Mundelein Seminary near Chicago. In addition to publishing numerous books, essays, and DVD programs, he is also the creator and host of *CATHOLICISM*, a groundbreaking, 10-part documentary series and study program about the Catholic faith.

Chapter 2
// Into the Light: Sharing the Spiritual Journey //
Jennifer Fulwiler

When I was in my mid-20s, I knew all about Christians. I knew that almost all of them were hypocrites who didn't practice what they preached. I knew that they tended to be uneducated people with few opportunities in life (hence their need to cling to fairy stories about deities and heaven) and that they foisted their beliefs on others out of a desire for control. Growing up in the Protestant South, I knew less about Catholicism but enough to have a pretty firm grasp on what it was all about: it was an archaic belief system run by men in the Vatican who made up rules to oppress people. Though nobody actually subscribed to the Catholic Church's archaic doctrines anymore, some people still called themselves "Catholic" just because they were used to going through the motions — but even these poor folks were made miserable by the Church and were always happy when they abandoned it for other belief systems.

This was the 1990s, when it was still easy for people like me to live life firmly implanted in a cocoon of ignorance. I had been an atheist all my life, even in early childhood, and had slowly but purposefully distanced myself from anyone who held religious views that weren't in line with mine. By the time I was out of college, almost everyone I knew was either an atheist or an agnostic. Of the handful of believers I knew, most were lukewarm about any kind of religious practice. In my social circles, conversations would start with the assumption that the other party subscribed to an atheist-materialist worldview. Jokes about Christians, sacred figures, and even God himself were perfectly acceptable. I could easily go weeks — if not months — without encountering a single person whose worldview differed from mine.

But that was all before the Internet.

In 2004, my first child was born. This was around the same time that it became popular for people to keep personal blogs, informal online diaries of their daily lives. Staying home with the baby left me isolated from my usual social circles, and reading blogs became a lifeline of human connection. The personal musings were so much more raw and relevant to my life than anything I could find in a newspaper; the ability to leave my own comment on each blog post allowed me to connect with each author in a way I never could when using other media. My stack of magazines seemed so flat and lifeless in comparison.

> *"The modern media of social communication offer men of today a great round table. At this they are able to participate in a world-wide exchange in search of brotherhood and cooperation. It is not surprising that this should be so, for the media are at the disposal of all and are channels for that very dialogue which they themselves stimulate. The torrent of information and opinion pouring through these channels makes every man a partner in the business of the human race. This interchange creates the proper conditions for that mutual and sympathetic understanding which leads to universal progress."[33]*
> — PASTORAL INSTRUCTION ON THE MEANS OF SOCIAL COMMUNICATIONS (1971)

I became increasingly immersed in this new type of community and quickly discovered an unexpected side effect of my involvement in this online world: my cocoon began to unravel.

The blog world was a deeply interconnected place. One blog post might refer to others elsewhere on the Web, the highlighted linked text enticing you to click and see what was on the other side. Each blogger also typically included a blogroll on his or her site, a public list of other people's blogs that he or she enjoyed reading. With no more effort than a couple clicks of a button, you could slide right outside your comfort zone. And, sure enough, more and more often I encountered new voices that I would have never sought out on my own.

Lost in this new web of people and ideas, I found myself face-to-face (or computer screen-to-computer screen) with Christians — only this time I couldn't so easily banish them with stereotypes. Here in this virtual world, where concrete ideas weren't buried under small talk and the awkwardness of personal interactions, I saw Christian beliefs laid out with a clarity I'd never encountered before. I saw spiritual journeys unfold before my eyes, at an intimate level that would have never been accessible to me in person. (People didn't tend to open up about the details of their personal relationship with God to loudmouth atheists.) Thanks to the anonymity inherent to the medium, bloggers let down their guard and shared more openly than they would in any other forum.

I was alternately baffled and intrigued, shocked and impressed. These weren't the ignorant, unquestioning people I'd concocted in my imagination! The stereotypes I'd attributed to Christians used to render them impotent to impact my life in any way; I could neutralize any tough questions they brought up by simply dismissing all Christians as a whole. But now I had to face the reality that thoughtful, educated people believed these doctrines — people who sought truth and questioned assumptions no less than my atheist friends and I did.

Providentially, this surprise discovery of the Christian online community coincided with an offline religious quest. Motherhood had inspired me to seek the truth more fervently than ever before, and I'd begun to notice cracks in the atheist worldview. I set out on a search for a belief system that explained not only the natural world but the human experience as well. I sought to find the best "box top" that explained the entire puzzle of the human experience, rather than just one aspect of it. After poring over stacks of books, I stumbled onto a path that took me to the last place I ever thought I'd end up: Christianity.

Had this happened 10 years earlier, I might have backed away from what I'd found. The discomfort I felt at coming so close to this belief system I'd looked down on all my life would have made it easy to get lazy, to let my religious search fade into the background of my busy daily life as a mom. But the blog world kept me engaged. I came to feel as if I knew the Christian bloggers I followed; I'd been sharing the ups and downs of their spiritual journeys with them on a daily basis, and this personal connection fanned the embers of my interest in this belief system.

In fact, I ended up starting my own blog. I was bursting with a desire to talk about all that I was learning but was too embarrassed to tell people I knew in real life that I was reading about Jesus. I needed an outlet for the overflow of my soul, and the Internet provided the perfect solution.

I recruited readers to come to my site by posting my blog address in forums where Christians and atheists debated, and soon I had a small but energetic group of readers from all different backgrounds. Knowing that I had this new platform for the exchange of ideas, my mind roared to life. As I washed dishes and changed diapers, my brain would be ablaze with all sorts of challenging questions about faith and God that I could pose to my readers. I wasted less time on television and vapid magazines and redirected my mental energy to the intellectual life I'd found at my blog.

The weeks turned into months, and soon my little website was packed with fascinating discussions. I wrote posts about every tough topic I could think of: "How could a loving God allow suffering?" "Why do you believe the Bible is divinely inspired?""What about the fact that so many Christians are hypocrites?" — all were common conversation starters on my blog.

As with most blogs, each post had a simple form at the bottom that allowed people to leave their own commentary. There were no complicated technical elements and no special logins required, so anyone who knew how to use a keyboard could join the discussion.

This new, completely open form of communication ignited an explosion of information, on my blog and in the world at large. The floodgates were wide open, with knowledge streaming in for anyone who sought it. And what I found was that, when you have almost infinite information and free flow of ideas, the truth rises to the top.

One morning an atheist left a comment in which he said, "There's not a shred of proof that a man named Jesus even existed!" I'd heard such statements countless times in my life, spoken in classrooms and coffee shops around my college campus. Nobody happened to have any historical tomes tucked away in their backpacks or purses to verify such a claim, so we all just assumed the proclamation to be true. Not so on the Internet.

No sooner had the atheist published his comment than two Christians responded with rebuttals, including links to their sources. They challenged him to read documents available online that cited the works of Josephus and other first- and second-century writers, as well as articles that addressed the authenticity of those works. The atheist could provide no such sources for his own claims and eventually admitted that he may have been in error.

Online Conversion Stories

"Spiritual memoir" has always been one of the best-loved genres in religious literature. These stories hold power because they are more than biography — they also offer spiritual nourishment. Discovering the reasons for another person's conversion helps stimulate our own faith.

For example, St. Augustine's classic *Confessions* recounts his transition from a distorted paganism to the Catholic faith. Blessed John Henry Cardinal Newman's *Apologia Pro Vita Sua* chronicles Newman's journey from Anglicanism to the Catholic Church. And *The Seven Storey Mountain*, Thomas Merton's autobiography, is a modern classic on spiritual rebirth.

While traditional conversion stories appeared in book form, the tools of New Media have made them much more widely available. Some recount their journey through podcasts or YouTube vignettes, while many others feature conversion tales on blogs, either in written or audio form.

George Sipe is one of these converts. His website, **Convert Journal** (www.ConvertJournal.com), features his own conversion story in four parts. In addition, his site links to more than 70 other conversion tales across the Internet.[34]

"People who are exploring Catholicism can find others with similar backgrounds and struggles," George says. "Their stories are encouraging and show potential converts that they are not alone. My list of convert stories focuses on those who are also bloggers, in order that their continuing journeys can be followed."

Blogging, in particular among New Media tools, has transformed spiritual conversion into a communal experience. Instead of reading about someone's conversion in solitude through a noninteractive book, blogs allow questions, reflections, experiences, and insights to be shared not only by bloggers but also by readers, through discussions in the blogs' comment boxes.

To see more examples of this dynamic, head over to the
Why I'm Catholic blog (www.WhyImCatholic.com). The site
features stories of converts from many backgrounds and
walks of life: agnostics, atheists, Hindus, Buddhists, and many
others.

In the 21st century, thanks to New Media, spiritual memoirs
are able to be absorbed and discussed as never before.

I saw this situation play out over and over again: someone
would toss out a half-baked argument against Christianity that
might have sounded impressive offline, but it would quickly be
demolished in the flood of facts provided by the Internet.

In this ruthless intellectual environment, where
misinformation and half-truths didn't stand a chance, I began
to notice something: there was a certain group of commenters
who had the best answers. They had the most information
and were the most fearless about tackling even the trickiest
questions. They loved science as much as we atheists did,
yet they also understood the emotional side of the human
experience better than anyone else I'd ever seen. It was as if they
had the secret owner's manuals to the universe and the human
soul. And here was the amazing part: they were all Catholic! As
many negative impressions as I had of the Catholic Church, I
had to admit that either these people were all super geniuses or
there was something special about their belief system.

I ordered a stack of books about Catholicism, many of which
I discovered from recommendations by readers of my blog.
Meanwhile, I began to read blogs by Catholics. If my stereotypes
about believers had faded after encountering the general
Christian blog world, they vaporized when I encountered the
Catholics.

The first (and most shocking) thing I discovered was that there are actually a lot of practicing Catholics out there. I could hardly believe my eyes when I read that some of the most insightful, interesting bloggers I'd begun to follow believed that contraception was bad and that the Communion host they received at Mass was the actual Body and Blood of Jesus. I could never have imagined that modern people believed such outrageous claims, yet I was intrigued by their reasoning. This discovery also expanded my horizons about Catholics: I hadn't known that there was an alternative to the type of "cafeteria" Catholicism where people pick and choose which doctrines to follow. I was intrigued — and more than a little inspired — to see so many people taking their faith so seriously.

Reading Catholic bloggers' explanations of this odd faith of theirs helped me understand it even more than the books I read: the blog posts were much shorter and easier to digest than the heavy books I was slogging through, and the ability to ask questions and receive a quick answer via the comment form allowed me to gain a deeper understanding of concepts that confused me. Through these interactions over my computer screen, I slowly came to see that the Church had a vast body of knowledge under its hood and that its reasoning for even the craziest-sounding doctrines was impeccable. In fact, I was starting to believe that it was the most reasonable belief system I'd ever encountered.

What impacted me the most, however, was simply getting a glimpse into Catholic life. I looked with longing at photos of glowing candles nestled in pine wreaths and rich purple cloths draped over tables as families celebrated Advent — even though I had no idea what an "Advent" was. Living vicariously through my favorite bloggers, I experienced the austerity of Lent and the colorful celebrations of Easter. As I watched their lives play out, I saw that this faith of theirs made them more alive in every sense of the word: they were more intellectually, spiritually, and emotionally vibrant than any group of people I'd ever encountered. I laughed as they laughed at the challenges of daily life — which were often far greater than challenges common in my social circles, since many of them had big families and little money. I read with tears of bewilderment and awe as they praised God through even the hardest circumstances.

Occasionally, I would accidentally click on a link to a secular blog when I meant to go to a Catholic blog, and almost every time I would instantly sense the difference. Even the most pleasant secular bloggers lacked a certain something — and it was something I only found among Catholics. There was an unshakable peace, a comfort with the ups and downs of life, an ability to handle all aspects of the human experience that I didn't see anywhere else. Once again, I was left feeling as if only the Catholics possessed the owner's manual to the human soul. Behind their natural human faults and foibles, they seemed strengthened by something that no one else had, something infinite.

One Billion Stories

All humanity, past and present, has yearned to communicate the spiritual journey through story. It seems that we're best able to depict the indescribable through drama, fairy tale, or narrative. The Church has a long tradition of this art, from Dante's journey through the afterlife to J. R. R. Tolkien's account of the Ring, to Flannery O'Conner's tales of Southern sin and grace.

Seth DeMoor recognizes the power of stories. Aiming to harness this power through New Media, Seth created the website **One Billion Stories** (www.OneBillionStories.com), with a goal of "listening to God's voice in the world." There are over one billion Catholics on this planet — over one billion distinct spiritual journeys — and Seth believes that each tale can inspire the spiritual journeys of others.

Armed with a backpack and a video camera, Seth rode his bicycle across the country, from Florida to Colorado, sleeping wherever he could find a free bed. Along the way, he filmed short interviews with all sorts of people, from young college students to religious brothers, from housewives to football players. Seth uploaded his videos to Vimeo, a video-sharing site similar to YouTube, allowing viewers to check in daily for new content. His numerous videos presented a fascinating tapestry of Catholic stories.

"Video has become the language of the Internet due to the invention of YouTube, faster Internet connections, and a generation raised on photos and film," Seth explains. "Therefore, One Billion Stories focuses on Internet-based video in its mission to evangelize the world."

Seth continues to post new interviews from current travels on his website. So far, he has uploaded over 300 of these videos.

As One Billion Stories shows, New Media can provide a voice to any person willing to share his or her spiritual passage. Blog posts and YouTube videos broadcast these tales throughout the world, allowing spiritual journeys — and personal stories — to intersect as never before.

All my research, combined with the witness of the online Catholic community, eventually won me over, and in 2007 I joyfully entered the Catholic Church. And as my blog continued, I learned that my story was not unique: I began to receive emails from men and women whose conversions to Catholicism were also due almost entirely to the Internet. They came from all backgrounds: atheists, Protestants, Mormons, and even Muslims. As with me, it was the combination of the availability of information and the witness of online Catholics that brought them into the Church.

However, in the subsequent years that I've been sharing my spiritual journey online, I've also received emails from people who have had a different experience. More than a few seekers have contacted me to say that they, too, were searching and were also overwhelmed by all the facts they found in the Church's favor, but they had different personal encounters with online Catholics. They came across blogs where the authors wrote in caustic, sneering tones, and belittled anyone with whom they disagreed. They came across online debates among Catholics where the people involved spewed vitriol at one another and showed an appalling lack of charity and goodwill toward their fellow members of the body of Christ. "If this is what Catholicism is, I don't think I want any part of it," one young person wrote.

My own experience, combined with the experience of so many readers of my blog, leads me to believe that we're at a tipping point in the history of the Church: the unprecedented ease of communication and access to information mean that now almost anyone who seeks truth can find it. Gone are the days when it's easy for people to remain isolated within the walls of ignorance. The Church has the truth on its side and is thus poised to win souls on a level never seen before in the midst of this information revolution. And yet, as I and so many others have found, it takes more than facts to win hearts and minds. It takes the witness of individual Catholics to show the world the person of Christ, rather than simply offering data about him.

When theologian Dr. Peter Kreeft was asked what he thought was the biggest obstacle facing orthodox Christianity today, he replied simply: "Our own sins…. Only saints can save the world. And only our own sins can stop us from being saints."[35] We shape society, and the amount of God's love we allow into our heart shapes us, he explained. We cannot expect a great renewal of faith in the world unless we begin to purge our own lives of sin.

This is timeless wisdom, but it has never been truer than it is today. Thanks to the flow of communication made possible by New Media, the Catholic world is no longer an insulated subculture accessible to only a few; it's now a public drama being played out on a grand stage. The windows of the Church have been thrown open for all the world to behold what's inside. So now, the critical question is: What will it see?

Jennifer Fulwiler is a writer as well as the "Director of Chaos Management" for her growing family, which currently includes four children under the age of 7. Her writing has been published in over a dozen publications, including *Inside Catholic*, *This Rock*, *Envoy*, and *Our Sunday Visitor*. She's been featured on EWTN Television, EWTN Radio, and the Relevant Radio network. She's also a columnist for *Envoy* and a regular guest on EWTN Radio's *Son Rise Morning Show*. In 2007, she became Catholic after a life of atheism. She's writing a book about her conversion experience and blogs about faith and the joy of the Catholic life at **Conversion Diary** (www. ConversionDiary.com).

CHAPTER 3
// Speaking Their Language: Connecting With Young Adults //
Marcel LeJeune

"Howdy!" This was the greeting my father and I received from *hundreds* of students at Texas A&M University as we toured the campus for the first time. A&M is a tradition-rich school, and one of my favorite traditions is the official Aggie greeting of "Howdy!" While I visited the school, I was overwhelmed by the hospitality of complete strangers who would look me in the eye and greet me as I walked past. I was quickly sold on A&M. And since graduating in 1995 with my undergraduate degree, I have kept a deep love for the traditions at my alma mater. But I am sad to say that "howdy" has died a quick death the last 10 years.

Why is "howdy" dead? Some blame it on the fact that the students in the Corps of Cadets (a military-inspired, student-cadet program) are no longer required to say "howdy" as they walk on campus. Others say it is due to the collapse of the Aggie Bonfire in 1999, which killed 12 students and resulted in a ban on an activity that once helped to unite the student body.

I certainly believe these factors contributed to the decline of "howdy," but the deathblow came from technology. When students leave class now, they immediately plug into iPods and cell phones. While they have these electronic devices on, they are shut out from the real world. Most current students won't even look at those passing by.

This attachment to New Media and electronic gadgets, and the resulting decline of person-to-person interaction, is now the standard for young adults. In fact, most do not know any other way of life. This means that the Catholic Church is facing a huge uphill battle to win the souls of young adults, who are more disengaged from the Church than ever before.

"The new digital technologies are, indeed, bringing about fundamental shifts in patterns of communication and human relationships. These changes are particularly evident among those young people who have grown up with the new technologies and are at home in a digital world that often seems quite foreign to those of us who, as adults, have had to learn to understand and appreciate the opportunities it has to offer for communications....

"Young people, in particular, have grasped the enormous capacity of the New Media to foster connectedness, communication and understanding between individuals and communities, and they are turning to them as means of communicating with existing friends, of meeting new friends, of forming communities and networks, of seeking information and news, and of sharing their ideas and opinions." [36]

— POPE BENEDICT XVI, MESSAGE FOR THE 43RD WORLD COMMUNICATIONS DAY (2009)

The Current Situation

Here are a few sobering statistics on Catholic young adults in the Millennial Generation:

- Only 40 percent of self-identified Catholic young adults are certain that you can have a personal relationship with God.[37]

- Sixty-four percent of Catholic Millennials attend Mass a few times a year or less.[38]

- Only 15 percent of Millennial Catholics go to Mass regularly.[39]

These statistics show the reality of the current situation and the problems we now face. We are no longer dealing only with Catholics who aren't formed well or who don't go to church very much. We are past that stage, as sad as it was. We have now entered into a post-Catholic age. The young adults who were raised Catholic will have to be re-evangelized by the smaller Church that is left once the demographic decline matures to fruition. The statistics show that our recent past has come back to haunt us, and the consequences are worse than what many ever thought they would be.

This crisis is compounded by the fact that the Catholic Church lags behind in reaching young adults where they are, because we have not embraced New Media as we ought to. This is despite young adults being plugged in, online, and engaged with New Media far more than any other generation.

Most individuals in the Church evangelize very little, if at all. But this laissez-faire attitude about spreading the Gospel will no longer suffice. We must reach out, engage, and evangelize our young adults or lose them to the secular culture or other non-Catholic groups.

Likewise, the Church is years behind the rest of our society in using New Media; and because young adults are some of the first users of new innovations, we must speed up our use of technology as a Church or we will continue to lose ground.

Some of the trends that we can look for in the near future include increased consumption of videos and social media (especially YouTube, Facebook, and Twitter), personalized marketing, and increased use of smart phones and other mobile technologies. These trends will dominate the way the Church either does or does not reach young adults. The changes in our culture are happening at such a dizzying pace that it is a wonder any one of us can keep up. But that is precisely what we must do.

A few items to note about some of the radical changes impacting how we reach out to the Millennial Generation:

- The most effective way of reaching young adults has now become Facebook. The traditional printed bulletin and pulpit announcements aren't nearly as effective, especially when most young people aren't coming to Mass.

- Young adults rarely use email. In fact, most believe its time is past.[40] Texting, Facebook, and Twitter are now the norm.

- Millennials are less likely to commit to long-term religious formation than previous generations. We must therefore be innovative in how we catechize them after we have them in our doors. The semester-long class is less effective than in the past, so short-term formation (e.g., Theology on Tap, guest speakers, etc.), blogs, podcasts, and other events that require no commitment or can be accessed at a person's leisure are more popular.

Busted Halo

Young adults have long been the most underrepresented demographic group in the Church. A 2003 study from the Barna Group concluded that "Americans in their twenties are significantly less likely than any other age group to attend church services, to donate to churches, to be absolutely committed to Christianity, to read the Bible, or to serve as a volunteer or lay leader in churches."[41] Though there are certainly other reasons for this situation, many young adults have become disenchanted with a Church that doesn't seem to speak their language or frequent their spheres.

Busted Halo Ministries (www.BustedHalo.com), supported by the Paulist Fathers religious order, is one group using New Media to reach this missing generation. Part of their strategy includes meeting young seekers on their own terms. In a country where only 15 percent of young-adult Catholics attend Mass weekly, while 72 percent of that same group uses social-networking sites,[42] Busted Halo focuses their attention on the digital world.

The site's "What Works" series provides spiritual direction by walking readers through different disciplines like "centering prayer" and "reading the Bible." The series also offers discussion about vices like gossip and revenge.

In terms of audio, the "Busted Halo Cast" podcast features over 250 half-hour shows that discuss spirituality from a young-adult perspective, while the "Facts of Faith" podcast includes answers to little-known facts and other pieces of Church trivia. Busted Halo also features dozens of streaming videos on everything from virtual pilgrimages to interviews and film reviews.

Busted Halo's "Church Search" feature helps young adults find local Catholic parishes that are known for being welcoming to young adults. This is an important feature as the Church seeks to use New Media to cultivate offline relationships.

Outside the main website, the ministry's Facebook fan page brings together young adults for support and encouragement on the spiritual journey. The Facebook page even includes a Lenten Slip Support Station for those needing encouragement after stumbling during their Lenten fasts.

If New Media is the language of young adults, then the Church must learn this vernacular. Busted Halo has become an expert New Media linguist, attracting, connecting with, and forming the spiritual lives of young adults.

Innovation

The Catholic Church does not change rapidly, and there are great advantages to our deliberateness. But in our fast-paced culture, we must learn to adapt to the needs of the individuals we are reaching out to. This does not mean a change in our teaching, but rather it is a response to the call for us to re-evangelize those people and cultures that were once Christian. Blessed John Paul II put it this way in *Redemptoris Missio*:

> [T]here is an intermediate situation, particularly in countries with ancient Christian roots, and occasionally in the younger Churches as well, where entire groups of the baptized have lost a living sense of the faith, or even

no longer consider themselves members of the Church, and live a life far removed from Christ and his Gospel. In this case what is needed is a "new evangelization" or a "re-evangelization."[43]

John Paul II has perfectly described the current situation in the United States today, especially with our young-adult culture. It is now our responsibility to go out and change this culture. It is our responsibility to reach out to young adults. It is our responsibility to find time to give of ourselves. It is our responsibility to use New Media and do what we can to raise up Catholic disciples for the future.

If you ever lose hope, then come visit where I work. I have now gone full-circle and work at St. Mary's Catholic Center at Texas A&M University, the largest campus ministry in the country. The last 15 years since I graduated from A&M have seen remarkable growth in our campus ministry, and here is some of the evidence that we are reaching this Millennial Generation at St. Mary's:

- We have 4,000-5,000 that attend Mass on the weekends.

- We have 10 scheduled times for Reconciliation, with long lines at most times.

- We have over 80 different student organizations.

- We have over 40 staff, including more than 20 on our pastoral team that I oversee.

- We have our own radio station, our own apartment complex, and more.

- We have graduated 132 priests and religious from our campus ministry, and there are over 40 more in formation. Each year, over the past 12 years, we have averaged more than 8 students entering formation for the priesthood and religious life.

- We are forming thousands of lay Catholics who are changing the culture. An easy example can be found by looking at the contributors to this book. There are five former students of Texas A&M who are contributors — Jennifer Fulwiler, Taylor Marshall, Matt Warner, Shawn Carney, and me.

Too often we have marginalized ministry to young adults. But we are losing generation upon generation of young people, and I can't emphasize enough just how dire the current situation is. *If the Catholic Church doesn't rapidly start to engage our young adults and evangelize them effectively, the Catholic population will begin to shrink very rapidly*.

As a response to this challenge to reach young adults, the staff and students of St. Mary's Catholic Center have been using New Media to engage our young adults. The results are impressive, even to me.

For example, we have always found it a great challenge to get our student population to register with us (we only have about 200 families in our parish, so we are primarily a campus-ministry parish). As every Catholic parish does, we ask regular attendees to register as parishioners. Most parishes will put out information cards, and some even have online registration.

But many people don't register because they don't want to go through the trouble. Some don't register because they don't want to be tied to a specific parish. Some have other reasons, but the net result is that a large percentage of those who attend Mass do not register. This is especially true of college students who never registered growing up, either.

To make things even more difficult, we have hundreds of students coming and going every semester. So keeping track of their data is very difficult. These factors meant we never registered a good number of our student population and never communicated very well with them.

To help fix this problem, we rolled out an initiative that has revolutionized the way in which we register and communicate with our students. Starting in the fall of 2009, we began asking students to bring their phones to Mass the first weekend after school starts. This naturally builds excitement and intrigue.

During the time for announcements, the priests have everyone take out their phones and turn them on — the first time any priest has ever done this, as far as I know. The priests then speak about our unity as Catholics and as a parish. They explain how we at St. Mary's want to know who the students are so that we can serve them better. All are then invited to register with the parish by texting us their name, email, and phone number. The whole process takes about three minutes.

Those without cell phones and those who don't have a texting plan (a small minority in a campus-ministry parish like ours) can fill out a traditional registration card, but one that only has name, email, and phone.

We then download all the registration information texted to us, before importing it into **flockNote** (www.flockNote.com, a creation of Aggie graduate Matt Warner; see Chapter 8 for more on flockNote). Next, we send them a message, via flockNote, to complete the registration process. This message asks for all of the other information we want to capture. When students complete the registration process, they are automatically entered to win one of several prizes appealing to college students (in 2010, we gave away an iPad, lunch with either our head football coach or head basketball coach, and many gift certificates).

After registration, parishioners and students can then sign in through flockNote and choose how they want to receive updates from St. Mary's (and from the different groups at St. Mary's): through email, texting, Twitter, Facebook, or any combination of New Media.

All individuals choose the way we communicate with them. Also, each student organization can send messages to those that register, if the registrants confirm that they want to receive messages from certain organizations. All individuals are also able to access their personal information through flockNote, so if anything changes, they can easily update it.

Besides registration, another hurdle we had to overcome was St. Mary's poor website. When I started working at St. Mary's in 2006, we were quite frustrated with our website. While the design was much better than the average Catholic website, it was not current and was hard to keep up-to-date because everything had to go through a single webmaster.

After looking for a solution to the problem, we partnered with a company called **eCatholicChurches** (www.eCatholicChurches.com). This company allows multiple administrators and contributors to make quick and easy updates to a parish website. It uses a simple interface and has allowed us to give student leaders access to each organization's page on our website. Our website is now well designed, up-to-date, and frequently used. We no longer have to rely on one person to update the website, and it is extremely easy to use, even for the person with average computing skills (you can find our website at www.AggieCatholic.org).

Spirit Juice Studios

When attempting to reach young adults through New Media, quality matters just as much as content. Regardless of a blog's excellent writing or the virtuous message proclaimed through a YouTube video, if the material looks bland or casually designed, young adults typically look elsewhere. As Pope Benedict XVI put it in his message for the 41st World Communications Day, "Beauty, a kind of mirror of the divine, inspires and vivifies young hearts and minds, while ugliness and coarseness have a depressing impact on attitudes and behavior."[44]

Spirit Juice Studios (www.SpiritJuiceStudios.com) shows how New Media can be both edifying and evocative. From attractive pro-life websites to moving videos and commercials, the design group brings a professional, contemporary style to Catholic media.

"Our goal is to create relevant, fresh, and captivating media," says Spirit Juice Studios cofounder Rob Kaczmark. "Typically, when you do that, you will gain an audience of young adults."

The Internet pours limitless amounts of content onto the computer screens of young people. Because of this, younger generations tend to be more selective of the content they consume.

"The younger the audience, the tougher the crowd," Rob explains. "For example, my mom can watch pretty much anything and say, 'Wow, that was nice.' However, with young adults, if they aren't captivated right away, they are going to just tune out."

New Media presents not just a utility but an art. As the second millennium's Renaissance blended artistic brilliance with religious symbolism, our third millennium's Digital Renaissance must do the same.

Using Technology to Further the Good News
We at St. Mary's Catholic Center at Texas A&M University use technology and New Media in many other ways as well. Below are a few examples:

- **Distance-Learning Equipment:** We are tied into our diocesan offices, which are located an hour-and-a-half away from our campus. This allows us to hold master-of-theology classes, trainings, and other diocesan-wide meetings, with large groups, without leaving town.

- **Podcasting:** We record all of our Sunday homilies and then upload them to our website for others to listen to.

- **Videos:** We incorporate videos into many of our marketing campaigns, programs, and classes. We also videotape guest lectures and upload them to the Internet.

- **Blogging:** Our Aggie Catholics blog (http://MarysAggies.blogspot.com) has become one of the most popular Catholic blogs in the country. One popular aspect of the blog is our "frequently asked questions" feature, where we have answered hundreds of questions, most of which have been sent to us by college students.

- **Facebook:** We currently have around 4,000 people on Facebook who "like" St. Mary's Catholic Center Facebook fan page (www.Facebook.com/AggieCatholics). The page has grown very rapidly and is one of the best ways to communicate with our young-adult population.

- **Twitter:** Our Twitter feed is the latest project we have undertaken (www.Twitter.com/AggieCatholics). It has already started to attract a number of followers.

- **Radio Station:** St. Mary's has a low-power FM station that covers the local metropolitan area — KACB 96.9 FM. We use the radio station to target young adults who are not involved in church. Our active students will listen regardless, but the station is also a way for us to evangelize. In addition, we podcast several of the radio shows on our website.

- **Tech Committee:** We have recently formed a technology committee which will help oversee many of the projects above, as well as help us plan for the future. This committee is made up of staff and IT/New Media professionals who can help us plan strategically into the future.

- **Electronic Giving:** Young people are giving less and less money in pew collections. They don't carry as much cash as older generations, so we have seen a quick decline in our weekly total. But we have compensated for this decrease by rapidly increasing our electronic monthly giving. This may sound foreign to many of us who grew up putting money in a collection basket, but if we don't start to be innovative in our practice of stewardship, we will start to see a quick slide in our bottom line.

- **Online Liturgical Schedule:** We had a local programmer write a scheduling program for our lectors, ushers, sacristans, etc. Each volunteer is sent an electronic reminder that they are on the upcoming schedule. If they cannot make it, they can inform the program, which will then allow others to go online and sign up to fill their slots (http://Liturgy.AggieCatholic.org).

The purpose of all of these initiatives is to reach out to young adults, engage them with New Media, evangelize them, and draw them closer to Christ. This is the call of the Church. This is our call as Christians. The use of New Media technology is just another way we can live out our calling to evangelize.

While many parishes and ministries might be behind in using New Media, we must quickly gain back the ground we have lost in the electronic mission fields. These are valuable tools, which bring unprecedented access to our fingertips at the press of a button. New Media uniquely gives the Church new opportunities to evangelize more people, especially the young. This is our call. We must answer this challenge, or we will lose the Millennial Generation.

Marcel LeJeune is a husband, father of five, and the assistant director of campus ministry at St. Mary's Catholic Center at Texas A&M University, the largest campus ministry in the country. He is author of *Set Free to Love: Lives Changed by the Theology of the Body* (Servant Books), in addition to having articles published in various Catholic periodicals. He is a regular on several national radio programs and has been featured on EWTN Television. Marcel speaks around the country on different topics relating to the Catholic faith. You can find him online at www.MarcelLeJeune.com.

// Part Two //

That the World May Know: New Media and Formation

Chapter 4
// Modern Epistles: Blogging the Faith //
Mark P. Shea

I ran across the phenomenon known as "blogging" in 2002, thanks to the labors of the magnificent Amy Welborn (http:// AmyWelborn.wordpress.com). She had been blogging about life from a lay Catholic perspective for some while before that, and I (who, just to give you some perspective, only acquired a cell phone sometime around 2006 and still don't know how to use 99 percent of the features) had been as typically slow to hear of or notice this blogging technology as I am to catch up with others.

The Attractions of Blogging

What caught my attention was not just the quality of Amy's work but the fact that the technology she was using to publish it was *interactive* with readers and that it was not subject to any editorial oversight but Amy's. This meant, in a nutshell, that Amy could speak as she pleased, with no editors to edit, no headline writers to change "Exploring the Mysteries of the Rosary" to "My Friend the Rosary"[45] — and that she could do so with a sort of familiar, casual conversationalism that is impossible to achieve in the pages of a magazine, book, or newspaper, for the simple reason that the reader can only respond via a letter to the editor a week or a month later.

That was greatly attractive for a number of reasons. First, it being the spring of 2002, the American Catholic Church was just entering into the "Long Lent" of the priest abuse scandals, which still cast a long shadow over the Church around the world. Lots of dumb things were being said in the media ("This horrible crime is caused by celibacy and an all-male priesthood!"), and it seemed to me that lay people with a reasonable working knowledge of the faith could speak to an American culture about the faith better than a priest could (since anybody in a collar was, at that time, being unfairly treated as an accessory to the crime). It also seemed to me that, with events unfolding so rapidly, it was important to be able to respond in as close to real time as possible. Blogging made that possible.

In addition, something else attracted and held me to blogging: the fact that I am an extrovert trapped in an introvert's job. I write for a living when what I would much rather be doing is gabbing with people.

I'm not alone in this. Charles Dickens, for instance, was much happier on the lecture circuit or in a pub or hanging around in the back of a crowd listening to the stories in the papers (especially his own) being read aloud to the public. Indeed, Dickens would actually get many of his ideas from the responses of the people reading his serialized novels in the English press. If they disliked what he wrote, he would change it (giving us, for instance, two endings to *Great Expectations*).

Now, as a Catholic writer, I'm not at liberty to give a new ending to the story of Jesus in order to please the consumer. But I deeply empathize with Dickens in his desire to get out of the house, get away from the writing desk, and get into some sort of good conversation with people. For me, the things I write spring from a deep desire to help people see what the Catholic faith has to do with their lives. That's because, as a convert to the faith, I have had a living encounter with Jesus that has liberated and thrilled me, and I love to watch as the lights come on for other people when they see how great the faith truly is.

So I realized that blogging has everything to do with why I became a writer and much to do with my personal makeup as an extrovert. It wasn't so much to write, as to teach, that I became a writer: to gab with anybody who would listen to what the faith taught, because what the faith teaches is beautiful, good, and liberating. I had turned to writing for the Catholic press because it offered the best forum for me to do that.

Now, with the advent of the blogosphere, I had an even broader forum — one that could reach anybody in the world with access to the Internet. And best of all, it was a forum where I could interact with my readers, getting feedback, argument, agreement, correction, new information, and new ideas for articles in real time. So I leapt for it, signed up with **Blogger** (Blogger.com), and in April 2002 launched **Catholic and Enjoying It!** (http://MarkShea.blogspot.com).

> *"Christ commanded the Apostles and their successors to 'teach all nations,' to be 'the light of the world' and to announce the Good News in all places at all times. During His life on earth, Christ showed himself to be the perfect Communicator, while the Apostles used what means of social communication were available in their time. It is now necessary that the same message be carried by the means of social communication that are available today. Indeed it would be difficult to suggest that Christ's command was being obeyed unless all the opportunities offered by the modern media to extend to vast numbers of people the announcement of His Good News were being used. Therefore the Second Vatican Council invited the people of God 'to use effectively and at once the means of social communication, zealously availing themselves of them for apostolic purposes."[46]*
> — PASTORAL INSTRUCTION ON THE MEANS OF SOCIAL COMMUNICATIONS (1971)

What to Blog About?

The motto of my blog more or less sums up what I'm about: *So that no thought of mine, no matter how stupid, will ever go unpublished again!*

For those interested in starting their own blog, this is a first clue about the difference in culture between the blogosphere and the traditional press. That is, a newspaper or a radio or TV show needs to sell beer and shampoo, be accountable to stockholders, not tick off the audience too much, and generally remain beholden to certain rules of the market; a blog, not so much. A blogger can pretty much blog about anything he or she pleases. If you care about politics, then you can vote to blog about that. If you love music, then tune your blog that way. If your interest lies in boxing, knock yourself out. If it's food, belly up to the keyboard and write about it! And if, like me, you are fascinated with how the Catholic faith illuminates everything from soup to nuts, then step out in faith and talk about it. It's your blog, and you can say whatever you want to. (However, this being a book about the Church and New Media, we will assume that you mainly wish to blog about the Catholic faith in some way, shape, or form.)

Even restricting the scope of your blog that much can still create vapor lock for some folks. Saying "Blog anything you like about the faith" can induce a sort of helpless paralysis because, ultimately, blogging about the faith is still blogging about everything since "Catholic" means "universal." It's a big universe: Where do I start? My suggestion: Start with whatever you'd say to a good friend about the stuff that interests you. In my case, I just jumped into the ordinary ebb and flow of stuff that was in the news, as well as my own burbling about whatever I was interested in or found funny.

So what if you aren't an expert? I'm certainly not. But you know *something* about *something*, and you have that in your pocket to start with. I happened to know a fair amount about things like Catholic theology and the experiences of a convert. So I spoke from there.

In doing so, I made it very clear that I was speaking not as a theologian, academic, pastor, or authority (that's for bishops) but as a reasonably well-informed layman. This matters because to talk about the faith is to enter into controversy and that, in turn, is to enter into our polarized culture and the demands of factionalists to choose their side and excommunicate "the impure." I studiously resist the impulse (endemic in the blogosphere) to virtually excommunicate. I have plenty of opinions about which *ideas* are and are not compatible with the Catholic faith, but I resist the demand to declare *who* is and is not Catholic. Such matters are (thank God) for bishops to adjudicate, not for me.

So while I will happily hold forth on the extremely dubious merits of an argument put forward by some Catholic on behalf of, say, the legitimacy of abortion or torture, I do not regard it as my place to say that a Catholic advocating theological or moral nonsense is "not really a Catholic." Nobody died and made me God. If the Church should excommunicate somebody (an event far rarer than lightning strikes), I defer to the Church's wisdom. But as for me, I think it is the business of laypeople to concern themselves with ideas, not with pretending to say who's in and who's out. I might say that a person holding a bad opinion or doing bad things is a *bad* Catholic, but then I'm a bad Catholic too. So, I'm not going to read him or her out of the Church when I have this big fat log in my eye.

The takeaway of this is: Focus on making your blog about ideas, not persons. The world has enough personal grudge matches. Don't add yours. Argue, by all means, but try to avoid quarrels. (And extricate yourself and apologize when you get sucked into them. I've had to do that a number of times.) If you are blogging about the faith, then try to make it more about the one, the true, the good, and the beautiful than about how much the world or Joe Blow stinks. That's not always easy, since the world does, in fact, stink, and the news every day is all about driving that fact home. But try to focus on Paul's exhortation:

> Finally, brethren, whatever is true, whatever is honorable, whatever is just, whatever is pure, whatever is lovely, whatever is gracious, if there is any excellence, if there is anything worthy of praise, think about these things. (Philippians 4:8)

Blogging: It Ain't World Peace, But It's Still Good

What blogging results in, for me, is a sort of betwixt-and-between kind of writing. It's not written for "the ages," any more than that chat you had with your Aunt Maude was the Gettysburg Address. Like most of our words, our blogging words may help people get through a moment of thought, curiosity, or doubt, in the way a Big Mac gets you through your hunger. These words can even be a sacrament of grace — which is always a delightful thing to discover, as when somebody emails you a note bubbling with gratitude for something you said (which you don't quite remember but which the Holy Spirit used to help them).

But by and large, I don't approach writing on my blog the way I approach writing a book. There's a certain quality of pub talk to it, a kind of breezy carelessness that doesn't tell lies but which has no problem telling tongue-in-cheek whoppers on occasion in the spirit of good-natured, tongue-in-cheek blarney. Of course, that doesn't mean there's no serious — sometimes quite solemn — conversation too. Often somebody will ask a question, and I will do my best to answer it, but I'll leave the combox (more on those in a moment) open for readers to add their two cents. Happily, information about the Church is abundant on the Web, and anyone seriously seeking an answer to a question about the faith is typically a click away from finding it — if they know where to look. You can help them if you teach yourself how to find the information. You can help them even more if you teach them how to find the information for themselves.

In addition, since blog conversation is so wide-ranging, it can bounce from careful exposition of some detail of the *Catechism of the Catholic Church* (when I am in teacher mode), to breezy backchat about something Senator Whosit said, to my (highly personal and non-magisterial) view of *The Matrix*, *Star Wars*, or the poetry of Gerard Manley Hopkins. Much of the time,

I feel like a combination of Statler and Waldorf, the two geezer Muppets who sit up in the box seats of the *Muppet Show* and make smart remarks about the antics they survey.

I spend a lot of the blog time watching the flotsam that passes by on the vast Amazon River of information called the Internet and spouting off about whatever happens to draw my attention. When I do so, I am typically giving not "the teaching of the Church" but simply giving the opinion of one lay Catholic about that new video, or about what that guy said, or about something a reader or another blogger wrote, or what occurred to me while I was in the shower. I try to keep it informed by the faith. But I also recognize that the faith does not exist to micromanage our views about which brand of toothpaste to use or to hand down dogmas about Nicole Kidman's acting skills, OK Go's Rube Goldberg videos, or the likelihood of contact with extraterrestrials.

In short, one of the chief attractions of the Catholic faith for me is how few things are carved in stone. By all means, learn the dogmatic content of the Catholic faith, and stick to it like a limpet — especially when people you care about (and don't want to disappoint) try to get you to cut corners on something essential to the faith "for fellowship." But remember as well that a lot of the faith is not dogmatic and that the Church does not function by the dictum "That which is not forbidden is compulsory." The rule of thumb is: "In essential things, unity; in doubtful things, liberty; in all things, charity."

To be Catholic is to be *catholic*, as in "universal." This means that everything relates to the faith because God is the Maker of everything. You can, says G. K. Chesterton, begin anywhere from pork to pyrotechnics and relate it to the Catholic faith, because the Catholic faith connects everything, including non-Catholic and even non-Christian faiths. The linkage is not strained but built right into the material under discussion, because God is

Lord of heaven and earth. And it is a faith peculiarly attuned to a medium which puts you in touch with just about everything.

This means that whatever I (or you) love (so long as we do not love it more than God) is something that is legitimate grist for discussion. So, in addition to talking about the faith and its relationship to culture, politics, what's showing at the Bijou right now and what's appearing on TV and other blogs, things that make me laugh are a very important part of the daily psychological diet. Therefore, my blog has always included a lot of stuff that is not strictly on topic but which just cracks me up. It also includes a lot of whatever other stuff I'd gab about with a friend: movies, music, or what I happened to be thinking about after the dentist made a remark about the kids today. But it's all looked at (as much as I can) from the perspective of a layman who believes the teaching of the Catholic Church to be true and who takes the *Catechism* as the normative expression of the Church's teaching. The title of the blog is, after all, "Catholic and *Enjoying* It," so my enjoyment of God's gifts of friends, family, and creation is at the heart of what I'm trying to say. Let what you love meet God — who is Love — and meet your reader's love too, and your blog will be a pleasure to read.

Popular Catholic Bloggers

In a certain sense, St. Paul was the original Christian blogger. His short, personal letters were disseminated to communities across the ancient world, inspiring comments and replies from all sorts of readers. Today, however, many in the Church approach blogging with suspicion, claiming that it's a shallow form of communication.

But that view is slowly changing.

"Although blogging has a reputation for being superficial," explains Catholic blogger **Eric Sammons**, "it allows one to address topics at some depth as well as engage in

constructive discussion with others about important topics"
(www.EricSammons.com/blog).

Citing blog discussions about Pope Benedict XVI's recent
letter on Scripture, *Verbum Domini*, Eric points out how many
subjects can be better understood when explored through
multiple bloggers holding different viewpoints and angles. In
this regard, blogging allows Catholics to more fully appreciate
the Church's teachings.

However, blogging does have its dangers, and Eric warns
about the risks of addiction, pride, and anger. "You should
only engage these New Media tools if you have something
definitive to say," Eric notes. "For example, if you simply want
to complain about the state of the Church, there is nothing
spiritually beneficial in engaging New Media, and in fact it
most likely will be spiritually harmful — to yourself and to
others. But if you want to tell others about how Christ has
impacted your life in a positive and charitable way, then
blogging offers wonderful opportunities."

When looking for good blogs, the hundreds and hundreds
of well-written options become quickly intimidating. To help
point people in the right direction, Eric compiled a list of the
Internet's top 200 Catholic blogs (www.EricSammons.com/
TopCatholicBlogs.html), ranked by the number of regular
readers. For a list of Catholics on Twitter, the popular micro-
blogging service, check out the website **Tweet Catholic**
(www.TweetCatholic.com).

Overall, the best way to discover good blogs is just to begin
reading some. Most blogs you read will reference and link to
other good blogs, opening you up to a world of great content.

It Takes a Village to Raise a Blog

The very nature of the Internet is interactivity. When
planting my blog, I decided from the get-go to both exploit the
connections I had and to make new ones with brashness. So I

emailed writers and bloggers I either knew or whose work I liked and said, "Hey! I've started a blog! Could you tell your readers?" There's no need to be shy about that. The worst that can happen is that the blogger or writer will ignore you. The best (and much more common thing) that can happen is that the blogger you contact will stick a link up (as is my custom) announcing "New blog!" and sometimes linking to something in particular you have written, thereby funneling his or her readership to you and providing you with your first readers. I have a number of readers who send me links to stuff they've written and who link stuff I write. Additionally, of course, you can use other social media (Facebook, Twitter, YouTube, etc.) to refer readers in those circles to your blog and build up your readership through the immense interconnectivity of the Web.

As you continue to blog, keep a little list in the back of your mind of other bloggers who might be interested in a given piece you've written and send them a link suggesting they might like it. The more your blog is present to the public consciousness, the more chances readers have to say: "It's that guy again. I liked his piece on 'Prayer and the Art of Motorcycle Maintenance,' so I think I'll check out his new piece on 'Underwater Basket Weaving and the Second Coming.' " The trick is to realize that readers develop loyalty to *writers*, not topics. If they come to like you, they'll read whatever you choose to write about, because they like you.

Care and Feeding of the Combox Denizen

A vital part of my (though not everybody's) blog is the combox (short for "comment box" — see Glossary). Different blogging platforms have different software available for these, and you can season your choice to taste, including having no combox at all if you like.

I installed a combox on my blog early in the game because (a) it became clear that I would be overwhelmed with mail if

I didn't and (b) a huge part of the attraction of blogging was the interaction with readers. I like hearing from people, and people naturally want to sound off about what they read, so comboxes were a natural. The basic rule of thumb I maintain in my comboxes is "Treat me and others as you would if you were a guest in my living room." This makes for lots of conversation and argument but also gives me leeway to boot out abusers, trolls, human toothaches, and sundry advocates of evil, terminal dumbness, or rudeness. If you aim to speak about the Catholic faith publicly, I can pretty much guarantee you will attract these people to some degree or other.

The basic procedure is common sense: for the large majority of your readers who are Normal People, my own suggestion is to take a pretty laissez-faire approach to the conversations that start up in comboxes. People can take care of themselves and generally know how to both advance their own views and defend themselves in conversation with critics. Don't nanny the conversations *too* much or else people will give up trying to talk if you jump on them all the time. On the other hand, do keep your finger (lightly) on the pulse so that conversations don't spin out of control and trolls don't suck all the oxygen out of the room with their domineering personalities that force quieter (and more profound and interesting) souls back into the shadows. That's more or less a skill learned by practice, like learning to ride a bike. But it can be done.

As to the fringe folks, warn troublemakers a couple times, and if they don't shape up, give them the boot. When you give them the boot, don't be intimidated when they write you in high dudgeon to accuse you of censorship because you aren't interested in their torrent of profanity, their theories about how wonderful and misunderstood Hitler's S.S. was, or their obsessive need to talk about their hobby horse and drag all conversations back to it.

It's your blog. You don't owe them (or anybody else) a public forum. Your comboxes are a courtesy to readers, not a sacred right for which our ancestors bled and died. You no more owe some strange troll a platform to spew about his obsessions than you owe a passerby a seat on your couch and at your dinner table. If you invite passersby into your living room and they abuse your hospitality by punching out your other guests and emitting a stream of profanity, you are perfectly within your rights to tell them to leave and, if they refuse, to shove them out the door and lock it. All of which is to say that a ban function is an indispensible tool for dealing with those folks out at the end of the bell curve who do not play well with others.

Blogging Clergy

At the 2010 annual gathering of the U.S. Catholic bishops, Bishop Ronald Herzog of Alexandria, Louisiana, encouraged his fellow shepherds to integrate New Media into their communication structures.[47]

Bishop Herzog cited three particular reasons why bishops should engage the digital revolution: the low threshold of investment, the opportunity for dialogue, and the speed of global New Media adaptation.

Many clergymen have already taken up Bishop Herzog's charge, especially when it comes to blogging. **Cardinal Seán O'Malley** (www.CardinalSeansBlog.org) and **Archbishop Timothy Dolan** (http://blog.archny.org) are two of the frontier blogging bishops, while **Father John Zuhlsdorf** (www.wdtprs.com/blog) and **Deacon Greg Kandra** (www.patheos.com/community/DeaconsBench) are prime examples of priest and deacon bloggers, respectively.

"Blogs and social media are a great way for clergy to connect with people — not just around the block, but around the world," says Deacon Greg Kandra. "I've been amazed at the readers and commenters that I've been able to collect over the years, from places as far away as New Zealand and the Philippines.

"From my experience, people are hungry for information, for inspiration, for encouragement, for connection," he adds, "and the blogosphere helps create community and spark dialogue among a wide range of people. It can also be a useful tool for evangelization, drawing the curious and the questioning into discussion." For more blogging clergy, check out Marcel LeJeune's list of blogging bishops (www. MarysAggies.blogspot.com/2010/08/Catholic-Bishops-Who-Blog.html) or head over to the **Catholic Blog Directory** for a comprehensive repository of clergy blogs (www. CatholicBlogs.blogspot.com/#priests).

Your Blog: Home Base and City on a Hill

One great thing about a blog is that you can test-drive ideas that you can expand in other places. It's a safe place among friends (by and large) who enjoy what you say and the way you say it. So you can play around on a blog and noodle new ideas or try out new jokes and see how they play. A goodly percentage of the articles I have written for other media have begun as conversations on my blog or as goofy conceits I have first drafted on a lark there.

If I find myself giggling or thinking "I never thought of that before! Cool!" that's a good clue that I should follow it up with some sort of polished version of the idea. Sometimes I will quote a remark by a reader and then comment on it, or spool the idea out a bit further in order to examine the implications. Often the dialogue that ensues will prompt me to write up my thoughts for one of the traditional publications I write for.

Sometimes I wind up quoting readers because something they say will illustrate a point I'm trying to make. (I mention on my blog that I observe the Welborn Protocol, which states that all correspondence is quotable unless the reader specifically forbids it.) So if you are interested in writing beyond the blogosphere, you can treat the blog as a sort of home base from which to launch out on further adventures in book or magazine publishing.

In the final analysis, though, a Catholic blog is above all a place to do what the apostles did: proclaim "the holy Gospel according to …" *you* in this case. This entails a twofold awareness. First, as a Catholic, you are bound by the solemn grace of Baptism to be a light to the nations by proclaiming Christ in accord with the life and teachings of Holy Church. In short, it is the Gospel of the apostles, not your personal preferences, that you are duty bound to speak when you are relaying what the Church actually says about X, Y, and Z.

But on the other hand, you are emphatically giving the Gospel according to *you*, just as Matthew, Mark, Luke, and John delivered their perspectives on who Jesus is and what he has done. It is perfectly acceptable for you to talk in terms of your personal experience of how Christ's Gospel and Church have affected your life with the Good News and the power of the Holy Spirit. The happy thing about this is that you don't have to be a genius or invent anything. You just have to know what the Church teaches (or where to find it in the *Catechism*) and teach the same thing, while doing your best to behave honorably and charitably. I speak not as a bishop or priest but as a husband, father, worker, writer, and ordinary schlub in the pew. Above all I speak as a sinner and prove it regularly by writing something stupid on my blog (got to live out the motto!).

The bad news is: You will screw up (as I do) while blogging. You will say something unjust. You will write in anger. You will fail to check a source adequately and state something bunk as fact. You will let your prejudices color your judgment. It's bound to happen. Welcome to the human race. But the happy news of the Gospel is that when you do, you have the power to say, "*Mea culpa*," and then to try to make amends by doing better the next time. So don't let that stop you.

You will still, of course, make enemies. But you will also, as you cooperate with grace, find friendship, love, goodness, fascinating new ideas, and the help of the Holy Spirit to grow in Christ. The most important thing a blog (or anything else in your life) can do is help you become a saint. The next most important thing is that a blog makes it possible for any Catholic in the world to live out, in ways unimaginable to our ancestors, the promise and command of Jesus, who told his Church: "But you shall receive power when the Holy Spirit has come upon you; and you shall be my witnesses in Jerusalem and in all Judea and Samaria and to the end of the earth" (Acts 1:8).

You heard the man. Get going! There's still a world to win!

Mark P. Shea is the author of numerous books, including the *Mary, Mother of the Son* trilogy, *Making Senses Out of Scripture: Reading the Bible as the First Christians Did*, and *By What Authority? An Evangelical Discovers Catholic Tradition*. He blogs at http://MarkShea.blogspot.com.

CHAPTER 5

// New Wineskins: Fresh Presentations of Ancient Tradition //
Taylor Marshall

If St. Paul lived today, would he use New Media? Would this great Apostle to the Nations have a blog? Would he upload his sermons to the Internet in the form of podcasts? I'm convinced that he would, for the simple reason that Paul understood how a message could be exponentially magnified through writing and word of mouth. As he wrote in his Epistle to the Romans:

> First, I thank my God through Jesus Christ for all of you, because your faith is proclaimed in all the world. (Romans 1:8)

When media specialist Douglas Rushkoff wrote his 1994 treatise *Media Virus* on messages "going viral," he was only reiterating what St. Paul had discovered almost 2,000 years ago. Briefly, "going viral" is the phenomenon by which unknown information becomes commonly known through a repeatable medium. In our age, messages can be spread quickly and broadly through email, blogs, YouTube, etc. Just as a virus enters a living body and then rapidly reproduces itself millions of times over, so also a message has the potential to rapidly reproduce itself within a culture.

For example, when Pope Benedict XVI speaks, his words can be sent around the world in under five minutes through electronic media. Within hours, his words can be on the pages of any newspaper or computer screen. What once took weeks to disseminate, now takes seconds.

The viral success of a story depends on the willingness of a potential audience to copy and paste that information through their own media outlets. Guided by the Holy Spirit, the Catholic

Church is arguably the greatest social-media success of all time. The Catholic faith proliferated throughout the Roman world by the Church's faithful preservation and proclamation of the message of Christ. Moreover, St. Paul is probably the first "viral" success story in antiquity. Never before had one person's letters been copied and disseminated as quickly as St. Paul's letters. The messages of Socrates, Plato, and even Aristotle never experienced the widespread success achieved by the writings of St. Paul.

> *"Surely we must be grateful for the new technology which enables us to store information in vast man-made artificial memories, thus providing wide and instant access ... to the Church's teaching and tradition, the words of Sacred Scripture, the counsels of the great masters of spirituality, the history and traditions of the local Churches, of Religious Orders and lay institutes, and to the ideas and experiences of initiators and innovators, whose insights bear constant witness to the faithful presence in our midst of a loving Father who brings out of his treasure new things and old (cf. Mt 13:52)."[48]*
> — BLESSED JOHN PAUL II, MESSAGE FOR THE 24TH WORLD COMMUNICATIONS DAY (1990)

St. Paul knew that to preach in person is best. However, he also realized that a letter read in a church assembly and then repeatedly copied is more effective in spreading the message of Christ. St. Paul explicitly encouraged this practice of reduplication in his Letter to the Colossians:

> And when this letter has been read among you, have it read also in the Church of the Laodiceans; and see that you read also the letter from Laodicea. (Colossians 4:16)

Although St. Paul did not use the term "media," he certainly realized that there was a desire and a demand within the Church for written documents that *could be copied and distributed.*

What seculars call "media," the Catholic Church has often denoted as "Tradition," and unlike the secularists, she zealously guards the deposit of faith as it is handed down throughout time. Similarly, St. Paul understood that his divine message was being mediated through others — both by word of mouth and by copied letters:

> So then, brethren, stand firm and hold to the traditions which you were taught by us, either by word of mouth or by letter. (2 Thessalonians 2:15)

The word for "tradition" in both Greek and Latin denotes the "handing over" of something. Paul relates that this handing over of Tradition is accomplished through means — words and letters.

St. Paul's perspective sheds light on the relationship between the Catholic Church and New Media. As a Catholic, I am interested in expanding the message of Christ to the ends of the earth. As a Catholic, I am also concerned that the Gospel that we share with the world through television, podcasts, radio, and blogs is *legitimately Catholic*. Without having personal one-on-one interaction with readers and listeners, there is already a certain risk of miscommunication. Moreover, every Catholic blogger should be keenly aware that he is not infallible and that he does not officially speak for the Catholic Church.

Traditionally, Catholic authors have submitted their books to the judgment of bishops. Books that are approved by a designated censor receive the *Nihil Obstat* (Latin for "nothing stands in the way"), and then the bishop grants an *Imprimatur* (Latin for "Let it be printed"). Currently, there is no sign and seal of approval for Catholic websites, blogs, and podcasts. Perhaps we might begin to petition for an *Imblogatur* ("Let it be blogged"), but until that happens I continue to seek ways to ground my online presence in the stream of authentic Catholicism.

How, then, can we remain confident that we are truly communicating *the* Catholic faith and not our *own versions* of the Catholic faith? My solution is to saturate my writings with Scripture and the Church Fathers — but especially the Church Fathers. If I am to write an article or post about the Sacrament of Baptism, I have to begin by admitting the following: Who cares what Taylor Marshall thinks? Instead I should ask: What did the great Fathers, theologians, and saints say about it? Therefore, I try to constantly glean authoritative passages from Church history.

My approach is rather simple, and those that read my blog, **Canterbury Tales** (http://cantuar.blogspot.com), know the formula. I typically raise a question and then provide an answer from the Fathers and Doctors of the Church. How is Mary the Mother of God? Let's take a look at what St. Cyril of Alexandria says on the subject. What will the Antichrist be like? Let's not speculate — let's turn to the holiest minds of the Church and look for answers. How does Baptism work? Let's read St. Ambrose for answers. How is the Eucharist a sacrifice? Let's turn to St. Thomas Aquinas. If your Protestant neighbor teaches, "Once saved, always saved," then how might St. Augustine answer him?

Podcasting the Faith

Centuries ago, when people wanted to hear a sermon from St. John Chrysostom, they had to be physically present, near his "golden mouth." Likewise, if people wanted to hear Fulton Sheen's radio show in the 1930s, they had to tune in to the right station at the right time.

Through the technologies of "podcasting" and "videocasting," however, these restraints have been lifted. A podcast is a series of episodic media files, usually audio, that can be downloaded and listened to at leisure, wherever and whenever you want. Videocasts are a subset of podcasts that feature video as their medium.

Podcasts feature content that is available for download 24 hours a day, 7 days a week. This allows you to carry lectures, radio shows, and video clips on your computer, iPod, cell phone, or almost any other mobile device. And you can play, pause, and resume the media as your time allows.

With new tools like podcasts, the Church is primed to offer her bank of wisdom in new ways. **SQPN** (www.SQPN. com) — short for Star Quest Production Network — is one of the most popular Catholic podcast destinations. The site features podcasts from all over the world, in multiple languages, covering a number of themes. Among their dozens of podcasts, you can learn about the saints through the informative "SaintCast," join with other moms through "Catholic Moments," or explore spirituality with other young adults through the "In Between Sundays" podcast.

You can also find solid Catholic audio and video through many other websites around the Internet. Two of the best are **Sonitus Sanctus** (http://CatholicAudio.blogspot.com) and **CatholiciCast** (www.CatholiciCast.com). Together, the two sites feature thousands of free audio and video clips. And each site allows you to browse its archives by topic or speaker.

Today, if you aren't near a radio when your favorite Catholic show comes on, you can stream it later through your cell phone. If you weren't alive while Fulton Sheen preached, you can now download his talks onto your iPod. And if you weren't near the Vatican to hear the pope's latest reflections, subscribe to the Vatican's YouTube channel and view them later.

Together, podcasting and videocasting have made the Church's ancient traditions more accessible and portable than they have ever been before.

Our questions need not be only theological. We might also ask this: How can we best keep Lent? We can then consult a number of sermons from the great saints on how to properly pray and fast during this time of penance. How do we pray? How do we repent and do penance? How do we create holy families? The saints have addressed all these questions, and their answers are profound. Our goal is to pose problematic questions and then consult the holiest minds and hearts in the history of the Holy Catholic Church.

In short, we are allowing the Church Fathers to do something new — we are allowing the Church Fathers to "go viral" through the electronic media. Their voices come alive again, and their words are read and heard by millions. As a Catholic author and blogger, I see myself as a research analyst. My task is to connect the right question to the right answer from the heart of the Church. At the end of the day, it doesn't matter what I think. It matters what the Church teaches.

As a Catholic, I enjoy the blessing of knowing that I will likely never be as holy or as intelligent as St. Augustine, St. Thomas Aquinas, or St. Alphonsus Liguori. This realization does not incite doubt or self-loathing. Instead, it frees me to turn to them for illumination. Their words are still with us, and we have much to learn from them. Their voices continue to echo whenever we open their books (or e-book reproductions).

With the prospects of New Media, we Catholics can "*media*te" the writings of the saints to an entirely new audience. Our duty is not to be infallible. Only the Holy Father possesses this extraordinary charism, and then only in certain carefully defined circumstances. No, our duty is to be a faithful communicator of those teachings that have been faithfully and consistently taught by the popes, councils, Fathers, and Doctors of the one, holy, Catholic, and apostolic Church.

To be faithful to the method described thus far, we must then raise a question and search out an answer from the Fathers. The question is this: How has the Catholic Church understood media and message? For the answer, let us turn to the fifth-century bishop of Calamensis, St. Possidius. Besides being a holy man, St. Possidius is known chiefly as *the* biographer of St. Augustine of Hippo, the latter of which is arguably the most important theologian in Catholic history.

At the conclusion of his biography of St. Augustine, Possidius summarizes the accomplishments of Augustine. No doubt, Augustine was a holy shepherd of the Church, a great penitent, a dutiful bishop, and a founder of monasteries and convents. The pastoral care and prayer of St. Augustine also yielded an increase in priests and a strengthening of the laity. However, it is Augustine's theological works — over 100 books — that Possidius cites as Augustine's greatest achievement. Through these books, Possidius claims that Augustine will continue to live. Possidius then cites a couplet from the tomb of an unnamed poet that reads:

> *Vivere post obitum vatem vis nosse viator.*
> *Quod legis ecce loquor, vox tua nempe mea est.*

> Traveler, know that the prophet lives after death.
> What you read, behold, I speak, for your voice is truly my own.

St. Possidius cleverly captures what we Catholic New Media users should be doing. Every time we faithfully reproduce the Church Fathers, "their voice is truly our own." There is great wisdom in this. St. Possidius echoes what St. Paul communicated at the beginning of this chapter. It is always best to be present in person, but when this is impossible, it is beneficial to *echo* the voice of others through oral and written means. When we echo and quote the Fathers in these new forms of communication, we are not only expanding the message of Christ and the apostles, we are letting their voice become our own.

Old Content, New Mediums

Religious masters have always encouraged spiritual reading and the study of theology. The more you know and contemplate God, they advise, the deeper your union with him.

For most of the past 500 years, books constituted the primary means for this spiritual study. To grow in faith, people would read a hardcover copy of Thomas Aquinas' *Summa Theologica* or Therese of Lisieux's *Story of a Soul.*

In the age of New Media, however, spiritual formation isn't restricted to books. Ancient teachings can now be passed on through many new technologies. Two of the most prominent examples are mobile devices and e-books.

Those with an iPad, iPhone, or other "smart" device can deepen their spirituality through all sorts of applications — "apps" for short — most of which are free or cost just a couple of dollars.

The "Catholic Directory" app uses GPS technology to find the nearest church, while providing Mass times, websites, maps, and directions to nearby parishes. If you want to pray the Liturgy of the Hours but can't imagine hauling around a stack of prayer books, check out the "iBreviary" app or turn to the "iMissal" app for the daily lectionary readings.

The "Recordatio" app places recent papal encyclicals on your device, while the "iRosary" app and "Confession: A Roman Catholic App" prepare you for prayer and the Sacrament of Reconciliation, respectively. And, of course, the Bible, *Catechism of the Catholic Church*, and the Catholic liturgical calendar are all available for download too.

Besides these apps, however, another new technology is becoming increasingly popular: electronic books. These digital texts — known as e-books — have exploded onto the scene in recent years. Amazon.com, the world's largest bookseller, now sells more e-books than paper books,[49] and their Kindle e-book reader is their most popular product.

The **Amazon Kindle Store** features more than two million out-of-copyright books that can be downloaded for free, as well as many must-read Catholic titles that can be downloaded cheaply (www.tinyurl.com/CatholicKindle). Cardinal Newman's *Idea of a University*, St. Augustine's *Confessions*, and the *Spiritual Exercises* of St. Ignatius of Loyola each cost less than a couple of dollars. Other websites, like **Project Gutenberg** (www.Gutenberg.org), **Saints' Books** (www.SaintsBooks.net), and the **Google eBookstore** (http://Books.Google.com/ebooks) offer hundreds of spiritual classics for free download.

Librivox (www.librivox.org), an audiobook website, is another rich resource with a bold goal: to make all books in the public domain available, for free, in audio format. The site features thousands of free audio books recorded by volunteers, ready for download to your computer or mobile device.

Overall, mobile devices and e-books are just two examples of how New Media can richly present old content through new mediums.

Most people will never seek out a dusty library, searching for what St. Augustine said about the Holy and Blessed Trinity. Most will not go through the trouble of translating the Latin of St. Bernard's words on the love of God. Even those patristic works made available in the vernacular are generally unknown to the vast majority of Christians. So, then, we have the joyful task of dusting off the manuscripts, cracking the spines of old books, translating fascinating texts, and then summarizing them in bite-sized morsels for the world. Best of all, it takes just a few clicks.

New Media links us to the Old Media of the centuries. The Communion of the Saints is not merely our memory of them and their powerful prayers for us; it is also our preservation of their words for all times and all places. Our Lord and Savior

Jesus Christ commissioned the holy apostles to be fishers of men. Although we are not apostles, we are blessed to have been given the biggest net known to man — the Internet. Let us cast into the deep. *Duc in altum* ("Put out into the deep").

Taylor Marshall was an Episcopal priest in Fort Worth, Texas, before being received with his wife into the Catholic Church on May 23, 2006. He is the author of *The Crucified Rabbi: Judaism and the Origins of Catholic Christianity* (2009) and *The Catholic Perspective on Paul: Paul and the Origins of Catholic Christianity* (2010).

Taylor is currently a Ph.D. candidate in philosophy at the University of Dallas, focusing on the natural law theory of St. Thomas Aquinas. He is a graduate of Texas A&M University (B.A., philosophy), Westminster Theological Seminary (M.A.R., systematic theology), Nashotah House Theological Seminary (certificate in Anglican studies), and the University of Dallas (M.A., philosophy).

Taylor and his wife live in Dallas, Texas, with their six children. He blogs at **Canterbury Tales** (http://Cantuar.blogspot.com) and **Called to Communion** (www.CalledToCommunion.com).

Chapter 6
// Digital Discourse: The New Apologetics //
Father Dwight Longenecker

My blog is a hungry beast. Readers visit the blog at least once a day, looking for the three "E's" — Education, Entertainment, and Enlightenment — and I have to feed them.

I try to provide what they are looking for with a conscious mixture of theological thoughts, current-event comments, inspiring anecdotes, controversial opinions, pretty pictures, scalding satire, prayerful ponderings, interesting links, solid apologetics, random rants, and contributions from my alter egos — "guest bloggers" who are a ragtag band of lovable (and despicable) eccentrics. The idea is for readers to share a slice of the fruitcake jumble of my life: evangelical, fundamentalist, Anglican, bibliophile, poet, Anglophile, American, theologian, Catholic priest, writer, father, film critic, husband, Pennsylvania Dutch, Southerner, sinner, and wannabe saint.

The blog's underlying intent is to provide an intelligent, positive, sometimes sharp but never dull defense, example, and explication of the Catholic faith. I am the first to admit that this "version" of the Catholic experience is particularly my own, but from the particular we move to the universal, and it is through my particular blog threshold that I hope readers will enter the fullness of the Christian faith within the Catholic Church. I'd like my blog to be the intriguing wardrobe through which the Pevensie children of this world might enter the wonderful Narnia of the Catholic Church.

And the magic seems to be working. Whenever I get tired of blogging or think I am only repeating myself and preaching to the choir, I receive personal emails and comments from those whose lives have been changed by my blog. They say things like "Father, please keep blogging. Your blog is the only

Catholic thing my teenage kids will read!" or "I hope you won't quit blogging. Your blog has clarified my thoughts about the Anglican Church and helped me take the step to swim the Tiber" or "I don't always agree with what you say, but I always enjoy reading it. You've made me think about the Catholic faith in new ways, and for this I'm grateful" or "Father, don't you dare give up blogging! Your blog is my first stop on the Internet every day, and you have made me laugh uproariously, gasp with wonder at the beauty of our faith, and you have given me thoughts to ponder all day long. Keep going!" So I keep going. Every day I try to upload at least one blog post, most days two or three. I feed the hungry beast.

More Christianity

As a tree is supported and nurtured by the roots, so my blog is supported and nurtured by the theory behind apologetics and evangelization. First, my journey with Christ began in a loving, Bible-based evangelical home. Our family's history was rooted in seven generations of solid, serious Protestant Christianity. This loving, gentle, and simple form of the faith provided a foundation on which, by God's grace, I moved through Anglicanism to finally being received into the fullness of the Catholic Church. On every step of that journey, I never saw myself as abandoning what went before. Instead, I was adding to it. C. S. Lewis famously wrote about "Mere Christianity." I wanted "More Christianity," and that desire for "more" brought me home to Rome.

> "The communications media — and we exclude none of them from our celebration — are the admission ticket of every man and woman to the modern marketplace where thoughts are given public utterance, where ideas are exchanged, news is passed around, and information of all kinds is transmitted and received."[50]
> — BLESSED JOHN PAUL II, MESSAGE FOR THE 26TH WORLD COMMUNICATIONS DAY (1990)

Secondly, most non-Catholic Christians do not disagree with what the Catholic Church teaches. They disagree with what they *think* the Catholic Church teaches. Also, Protestants' theological viewpoints are most often determined by what they deny rather than what they affirm. For example, as an evangelical Christian, I was not certain what I believed about the Lord's Supper, but I knew what I didn't believe: I didn't believe that the bread and wine became the body and blood of Christ. The process of moving from Protestant to Catholic begins with the desire to have a genuinely open mind and to be fair to the Catholic faith. G. K. Chesterton wrote that once a man starts being fair to the Catholic faith, it is not long before he is attracted to it.

The third theoretical point is that I am not convinced that many souls are won by argument. It is famously said about apologetics that you can win an argument and lose a soul. The apologetics on my blog are woven into a much bigger picture of Catholicism. I want the reader to glimpse the power and the glory of the Catholic Church, but I also want them to glimpse the humanity and humor of being Catholic. In other words, I want them to glimpse the art of being Catholic — not just the argument for being Catholic.

The foundation for apologetics on my blog is therefore linked with these three ideas: first of all, I want the reader to be attracted to the "more" of Catholicism. This is why I post pictures of magnificent monasteries, quotes from the Church Fathers and saints, explanations of Catholic devotions, YouTube clips of Catholic music, poetry by priests, passages from the *Catechism*, explanations of liturgical detail, and beautiful Catholic art and architecture. I want the non-Catholic reader who already loves Jesus to imagine how much bigger and more beautiful that love for Jesus could be within the Catholic faith.

Secondly, if the reader has come to the blog at all, he is open minded enough to read a blog by a Catholic priest. Once he's there, I want him to find a mind and a heart that is open and joyful and bright and free. I want to present a clear and uncompromising Catholic faith, but I don't want to hit the reader with the kind of sourness, self-righteousness, and condemnation too often found in conservative Catholic circles. Through the blog, I want to encourage the quest for truth, not shut it down with instant answers. I want to welcome that open mind and use the combox (comment box) to stimulate debate and push the inquirer to ask more questions.

Thirdly, while I encourage debate and comment, I try not to engage in detailed theological "I'm right, you're wrong" debate with non-Catholics. I discourage "Bible proof text shoot-outs." There is a place for this sort of debate, but it's not on a blog. Instead, in all the ways described, I aim to present the reader with the "More Christianity" of the Catholic faith. I want them to see the big picture, to open wide the doors to Christ, and to be expansive in their vision.

Called to Communion

In his apostolic letter *Novo Millennio Ineunte* ("At the Beginning of the New Millennium"), Blessed John Paul II called for a "new evangelization."[51] This evangelization was to breathe fresh life and a renewed spirit into the world, particularly into those countries and communities that were once Christian but whose faith had dwindled.

One facet of the pope's call was a revival of apologetics. The third millennium saw the advent of the Internet, which opened the door for this apologetical revolution. Quality explanations of Church teaching could be found by anyone using a search engine. Writings from the early Church Fathers and saints through the ages were available for free on the Web. And intelligent, serious theological discussion began happening across comment boxes, blogs, and chat rooms.

Called to Communion (www.CalledToCommunion.com) has quickly become one model of this "new apologetics." The website, created by a handful of converts from Reformed Protestantism to Catholicism, aims to effect reconciliation and reunion between Catholics and Protestants. The site moderators see the Internet as a powerful way to move toward this goal.

"The Internet adds a new dimension to evangelization and opens new doors for interfaith dialogue," explains Tim Troutman, editor in chief at Called to Communion. "Even a decade ago, it might have been possible for the average Protestant to remain in a closed circle of familiar ideas and arguments. With the Called to Communion website, we're able to help expose large numbers of Protestants from all over the world to Catholic thought and solid arguments for the Catholic faith."

The Called to Communion podcast features lectures from some of the brightest theologians across the globe. A recent series of talks explored two Marian dogmas — the Immaculate Conception and the Assumption — by explaining the biblical, historical, and theological basis for such teachings.

Practicing the advice in Pope Benedict XVI's encyclical *Charity in Truth*, the website maintains strict comment guidelines to ensure charitable dialogue; hostility is not welcome on the site.

"Our comments are moderated and all comments must adhere to our posting guidelines," says Tim. "Consequently, Called to Communion is recognized even among Protestants as a place to conduct civil dialogue on these important (and often touchy) issues."

This combination of serious apologetics and charitable discussion has led a number of the site's visitors to seriously consider the claims of the Catholic Church, while a handful have even made the full swim across the Tiber.

Through their work, Called to Communion is answering Pope John Paul's call for a revived apologetics.

Communicating Clearly

A blog communicates with ordinary people within the daily routine of their ordinary lives. The best blog post is short and sweet. It is quick communication for the instant age. Therefore, the classic rules for communicating clearly are more important than ever. One of the toughest things to do is to take abstract, intellectual concepts and make them accessible for the ordinary reader. C. S. Lewis used to give instruction to theological students on how to do this. Underlying his specific rules was the foundational concept of good communications: Serve others. Write for the reader — not for yourself.

The specific rules for clear communication in the religious realm are to avoid highbrow intellectual language. Don't write about "the consubstantial one-ness that exists within the Divine inter-relatedness." Instead, write about "the beautiful unity that lies at the heart of God himself." Use homey illustrations, and say "that unity is like the unity between a loving husband and wife."

And avoid highbrow intellectual references. You don't need to tell people that your quote is from Dostoyevsky or Jean Paul Sartre. That makes them feel as if you are smarter than they are and that you are showing off. Just say, "As someone has written...." You should also avoid theological, ecclesiastical, and liturgical jargon. No need to spend a lot of time discussing the historical significance of the be-ribboned maniple or the fascinating details of the Cappadocian Fathers' understanding of the Filioque clause. Speak about everyday things.

At the same time, the apologist striving for clear communications cannot dumb down the content or patronize the reader. Your reader is not stupid. He's just not had the same education you have. You might know more about religion. He probably knows more about something of which you are ignorant. Respect the reader. When you explain something, assume he already knows it but just wants to be reminded. Even if he doesn't know it, he'll thank you for assuming that he does.

Finally, clear communication is always passionate. The beauty of the blog is that a writer can say whatever he wants in whatever way he wants to say it. The blogger can speak from the heart, and a blog is best when he does so. Remember, the word "enthusiasm" comes from the words *en theos*, meaning "God within." Writing with a fire in your heart and a love for your topic means that you will find yourself living out Blessed John Henry Newman's motto: "Heart speaks to heart."

Online Apologetics

Though some commentators have decried the Internet's "information overload," the world of online apologetics has benefited from this treasure chest of content. The Internet offers a giant collection of articles, source documents, and electronic books explaining many of Christianity's most misunderstood teachings.

When it comes to online apologetics, one of the best informational resources is the **Catholic Answers** website (www.Catholic.com). There you can listen to live or archived radio shows, download a frequently updated podcast, browse an online Catholic encyclopedia, and explore one of the largest apologetical libraries in cyberspace. Almost all of the site's content is arranged by topic — with the whole website searchable — making it easy to find the answers or explanations you are looking for.

Another impressive feature of the site is the discussion forum. Since its inception, the forum has seen over 450,000 different discussion threads with over 7.5 million posts. All sorts of topics are discussed, from ecumenism to liturgy, apologetics to prayer. And with over 200,000 members, the forum is the largest Catholic community on the Internet.

In addition to big groups like Catholic Answers, individual apologists are taking advantage of New Media as well. **Patrick Madrid** (www.PatrickMadrid.com) has long been one of the leading defenders and promoters of the Catholic faith. He has written many books on apologetics, spoken to thousands of crowds across the country, and discusses Catholic teachings on his radio show.

Though Patrick has long used these older mediums, the "digital continent" has allowed him to bring his gifts to a much wider audience. Readers of Patrick's blog will find biblical resources on different spiritual topics, links to informative articles, and commentary on current events.

Patrick also interacts with readers through his Facebook page.[52] There he provides answers to questions on Catholic teaching, offers prayer to those in pain, and once even asked suggestions for future book topics, drawing in hundreds of responses.[53]

As seen in both of these cases, New Media has opened the floodgates to religious information. For those defending, promoting, or learning about the faith, it has never been easier to find information and answers to many difficult questions.

Personally Universal

The word "blog" comes from "web log." The blog started in the late 1990s as a way for an individual to keep a personal journal online. The idea that it would attract a wide readership was alien to the original concept. But what is written is intended to be read, and so web logs took off as a novel way of instant, individual communication.

The most successful blogs continue to be faithful to the original format. There are group blogs and corporate blogs and commercial blogs, but the real genius of a blog is that one individual chronicles his enthusiasms, ideas, thoughts, and perspectives on life and that other individuals choose to share these things with him. The blog is an outgrowth, therefore, of the old-fashioned editorial columns, in which newspaper readers checked in every day to see what their favorite columnist had to say.

This is the true strength of the blog: that the blogger's individual voice can find a platform. This personal touch is also free of editorial control, commercial pressures, and financial anxieties. A newspaper columnist has to be aware of his editor always hanging over him. He has to be aware of commercial realities, and he can't afford to offend his sponsor. What he writes may affect his paycheck. The blogger has none of these anxieties and pressures. Because he blogs for free, he can say what he wants. Furthermore, because of the technology he can say what he wants instantly (and if he regrets what he has written, he can delete the post or edit it later).

This personal aspect to blogging is enhanced with the fact that, through the comment box, the readers can also respond instantly. And the instant response you get from readers is one of the most fun parts of blogging: "What, you mean someone out there is actually reading what I'm writing! How cool is that!!??" Before long, a personal relationship builds up between blogger and reader. A community develops, and regular readers and commenters interact in the combox along with the blogger.

Blogging is not only personal, but it is also universal. You can get a gadget for your blog that not only charts the number of readers you have but also where they come from. I can check my counters and see that I have readers from nearly 200 countries; 63 percent come from the United States, and the others from around the world. Blogging therefore presents us with an amazing new capability. Through a blog, one individual has the capacity for instant, global communications. For the priest blogger, this means instant, global apostolic evangelization.

Devin Rose

The Internet explosion has allowed anyone with a computer to offer his or her own explanations, definitions, or interpretations of Christianity. This makes it difficult to determine whether an article is accurate, especially when it concerns the Catholic Church. While the Internet holds many faithful depictions of the Church, plenty more are distorted, partial, or just plain wrong.

The primary way people discover facts in the digital world is through search engines like Google, Yahoo!, or Bing. But the top search results for a particular topic aren't necessarily the most accurate, just the ones that have been clicked on the most.

When exploring Catholic teachings, it's fairly common that the top search results will come from non-Catholics seeking to discredit the Church. You might find a Protestant describing the Eucharist as cannibalism, or an atheist depicting believers as deranged, cultish sadists. These false depictions run rampant across the Web.

Blogger **Devin Rose** (www.DevinRose.HeroicVirtueCreations. com/blog) recognized this dilemma. "If Catholics are not in the top search results for important phrases pertaining to the faith, we lose out on a critically important means of evangelization," Devin says. "Instead, other groups and people will draw those searchers to their own sites, and they will miss out on hearing the fullness of the truth of Christ."

As a remedy, Devin began creating videos on Catholic apologetics, addressing the most popular search phrases on Google. From the question "Are Catholics Christians?" to "Do Catholics Worship Mary?" Devin wanted to provide accurate answers to popular questions.

"I created a video that targeted one of those key phrases and was amazed to discover that just days later, when I searched for that phrase, my video appeared in the top 10 results! That demonstrates to me two things: first, there is a great need for more Catholics to create such content, and second, there is an easy opportunity to dominate search results of key phrases."

In addition to these videos, Devin also has a podcast where he similarly explains Catholic doctrine. He shares the story about a man from Albania who found his apologetics podcast by chance, and through listening the man became convinced that the Catholic Church held the fullness of truth. The man knew that in his culture, becoming Catholic would mean a loss of income and friends. Nonetheless, he exchanged regular emails with Devin and became so convinced of the Church's claims that he began translating Devin's podcast into his native tongue, sharing his discoveries with others.

Without New Media, this exchange never would have occurred. But with these new technologies, Devin has become what Pope Benedict XVI calls a "digital missionary," bringing truth to the online world.

It is this combination of personal and universal which has such great capacity to change lives, and why, as a Catholic priest, I have heeded the call of the Holy Father for priests to be involved in New Media.

When I receive a comment from the Philippines clarifying a point I made, thanking me for a post, and asking for prayer, I'm sharing in the work of the apostles. When a reader from Brazil asks me to pray for his dying mother and seeks comfort from a priest, I'm able to respond and offer what help I can. When a teenager from Wisconsin who is struggling with same-sex attraction wants to talk, I can spend a few moments with him while connecting him with a counselor in a nearby town. When an Anglican priest in England writes to tell me that he was received into full communion with the Catholic Church, and that my blog helped guide the way, I have cause to rejoice. Or when an evangelical student asks if he can stop by to see me as he's traveling through my state, and he ends up becoming a Catholic and heading off to seminary, I realize that the blog may be a hungry beast, but it is also an amazing and indescribable beauty.

Father Dwight Longenecker is the parish priest of Our Lady of the Rosary Parish in Greenville, South Carolina. He also serves as chaplain to St. Joseph's Catholic School. He is the author of 12 books on the Catholic faith, apologetics, and spirituality. He writes for **Beliefnet** (http://www. Beliefnet.com) and blogs at **Standing On My Head** (http:// gkupsidedown.blogspot.com).

// Part Three //

Fostering the Flock: New Media and Community

CHAPTER 7

// Innovative Shepherding: New Media in the Diocese //
Scot Landry

On July 1, 2010, Cardinal Seán O'Malley, O.F.M. Cap., established the Catholic Media Secretariat in the Archdiocese of Boston. This action instituted into the organizational structure of the archdiocese a group whose purpose is to implement the Holy Father's call to extend the Church's evangelization efforts into the "digital continent."

Cardinal O'Malley's desire is to put all forms of media, old and new, at the service of the primary mission of the Church, which is to share the Good News of Jesus Christ with the world. Our group wants everything the Church knows and believes about God to be shared with everyone, everywhere — on demand, through the power and promise of Catholic media. Additionally, we hope that our efforts in Catholic media will strengthen the connection Catholics in the Archdiocese of Boston share with their shepherd and with one another, promoting a stronger communion within our one local Church.

Distributing Catholic Media Content

One of our important goals in our Catholic Media Secretariat is to include every possible media platform. This allows us to take content produced in one media platform and integrate its message to other platforms and extend its reach. We are blessed to have all the major media communication types within our secretariat:

- **Television and Video:** CatholicTV® (formerly Boston Catholic Television) is the oldest Catholic television network in the United States and presently the second-largest national Catholic network, with EWTN the largest. Catholics can watch formational videos on demand through CatholicTV.com and our several YouTube and Vimeo channels.

- **Newspaper:** The *Pilot*, established in 1829, is America's oldest Catholic newspaper and the official newspaper of the Archdiocese of Boston. Its website, PilotCatholicNews. com, has earned several national awards for the presentation of Catholic news online.

- **New Media:** Our Pilot New Media group manages BostonCatholic.org (the official website of the Archdiocese of Boston), many other websites (parishes, archdiocesan initiatives, ministries, and schools), and official Facebook, Twitter, Flickr, YouTube, Vimeo, and UStream presences for the archdiocese.

- **Printed Parish Communications:** Our Pilot Bulletins and Pilot Printing groups allow us to print parish bulletins, annual reports, newsletters, and promotional materials.

- **Diocesan Directory:** Our Pilot Catholic Directory compiles all the official information of all institutions within the Archdiocese of Boston.

- **Radio and Audio:** Our Catholic Radio Apostolate interacts with the Station of the Cross, WQOM 1060-AM, which launched on All Saints' Day 2010. Our Catholic Media Secretariat soon will begin broadcasting a daily program on WQOM. The station's strong 50,000-watt signal reaches the entire Archdiocese of Boston.

Assisting Catholic Institutions and Leaders

Our Catholic Media Secretariat also exists to extend the evangelization and communication goals of other Catholic ministries and leaders. For example, we assist Cardinal O'Malley with his blog (www.CardinalSeansBlog.org) and with his weekly email message. These are two primary ways Cardinal O'Malley directly communicates with Catholics throughout the Archdiocese of Boston.

We also help other diocesan agencies and ministries by widely distributing their content through the use of New Media vehicles, such as websites, social media, and online video presentations.

Priests, deacons, and other pastoral ministers can extend their ministry through New Media ventures. We help them set up their own websites, blogs, social media, and email so that they can effectively connect with fellow parishioners.

The secretariat sets a high priority on parishes and parochial schools regarding our New Media efforts since parishes are the primary location for learning and living our faith in community. We help parishes establish a welcoming, current, and strong presentation of their ministries and faith life through websites, social-media engagement, and weekly bulletins.

This type of grassroots involvement has convinced us that for maximum impact, New Media needs to be embraced at the parish level. A recent study we conducted on parish usage of websites, email, Facebook, and blogs in the archdiocese revealed a tremendous opportunity for improvement. The study showed that only 31 percent of our parishes have a website with good appearance, content, and functionality. Further, it indicated that only 23 percent of our parishes utilize their website domain for staff emails; many parishes are now welcoming our offer to help fix this by transitioning to a Google Applications platform for email and calendar. Regarding the use of social media and blogs, we found that only a few parishes have a Facebook presence or blog linked to their parish websites.

Many parishes and priests have already responded to our programs and have initiated improvements. They have seen how a little support and guidance can quickly connect them to their New Media-savvy parishioners.

"Recognizing the validity, and indeed the urgency, of the claims advanced by communications work, bishops and others responsible for decisions about allocating the Church's limited human and material resources should assign it an appropriate, high priority, taking into account the circumstances of their particular nations, regions, and dioceses."[54]

— PASTORAL INSTRUCTION ON SOCIAL COMMUNICATIONS (1992)

"Social media are the fastest-growing form of communication in the United States, especially among youth and young adults. Our Church cannot ignore it, but at the same time we must engage social media in a manner that is safe, responsible, and civil."[55]

— USCCB SOCIAL MEDIA GUIDELINES (2010)

Helping Catholic Organizations Embrace New Media: The "7 E's"

Embracing New Media obviously involves embracing new technology. Technology-adoption patterns have been thoroughly studied by many technology firms and business schools. Perhaps the most famous data comes in the form of the "Rogers Adoption Curve," which holds that in general society, 2 percent are innovators, 14 percent are early adopters, 34 percent are in the early majority, 34 percent are in the late majority, and 16 percent are laggards in adopting new technology.

No study has been done on Church leaders, but my experience working in the Church allows me to posit that we have far fewer innovators and early adopters of technology relative to the general society, and far more in the late majority and laggard categories. My estimate would be that within the Church, only about 1 percent of us are innovators, 9 percent early adopters, 20 percent early majority, 30 percent late majority, and 40 percent laggards. This is ironic, given that the Church throughout its history has been an early adopter of technologies like the printing press, television, and radio.

What can we do about this slow New Media adoption curve? In the Archdiocese of Boston, we describe our work using the "7E's." Much of our initial work is to *Educate*, *Encourage*, and *Expose Excellence* in order to motivate Church leaders to embrace these new technologies. After they commit to using these tools, we help them *Evaluate* their current efforts and *Execute* new approaches.

Finally, once the new tools are operational, we help *Extend* their content across other platforms before helping them gauge how well they are furthering their primary mission to *Evangelize* — not just share information.

- **Educate:** Through our presentations, seminars, webinars, blogs, YouTube training videos, newspaper columns, and one-on-one witness, we inform every Church leader of Pope Benedict's and Cardinal O'Malley's call to adopt New Media. We explain how every one of the Church's media vehicles is a "virtual front door" to the Church and that it should be welcoming, well cared for, and worthy of someone's visit. For example, if a parish church had a dilapidated front door with graffiti on it and a broken sign with outdated Mass times, many that might otherwise want to stop in for a visit might keep on moving. Similarly, New Media vehicles that are out-of-date, out-of-style, and don't warmly welcome newcomers and encourage them to become regular visitors miss a big opportunity.

- **Encourage:** Here we help Church leaders commit to launching improvements to current vehicles, such as their website or email system, and to adopt new tools such as Facebook, blogs, and videos. We share with them how important it is for our Church to make Christ present to everyone everywhere, and we try to show them how the New Media launch process is almost always straightforward and cheap. To emphasize New Media's importance to Church leaders, we explain that their "outpost" on the "digital continent" might just be what the Holy Spirit uses to bring someone back to a deeper relationship with Christ and His Church.

- **Expose Excellence:** People like to see examples of what others are doing. When a pastor sees a beautiful parish website, or observes how a fellow priest's impact expands with a blog, or notices how a Facebook presence connects a parish with young adults and contributes to a more active community, he is more likely to follow those templates for himself and his parish. To inspire other parishes and leaders, we share examples of excellence in our presentations, seminars, and webinars. We also plan to create an annual series of "Archdiocesan Media Awards" to recognize those parishes, schools, and ministries that are excelling in their evangelization of the digital continent.

- **Evaluate:** We provide tools to make it easy for parishes to calibrate their current status and possible stages of improvement. Many parishes prefer to enhance their media vehicles one level at a time versus a total overhaul, so we assist them at their desired pace. This evaluation stage is crucial before executing new endeavors.

- **Execute:** For those who are new to technology, there is often a fear of the unknown and a myth that the development of New Media is hard and expensive. But once a leader or organization knows what it wants to accomplish (e.g., "a website that looks like St. Agnes' website"), our office can either help them build it or recommend third-party firms (we have a list of approved providers which have provided good services and prices to other Catholic organizations). Also, while working with Church organizations, the archdiocesan media groups share the USCCB norms for the use of social media and for communication with minors.[56] We recommend that dioceses also publish their own norms to expand on those from the USCCB.

- **Extend:** Many leaders are concerned that creating content for the New Media platforms they launch will take too much time. We help them identify what they currently do that can be deployed into other platforms. In our diocese, CatholicTV® programs can be placed directly on parish websites through the CatholicTVjr™ widget, which is available to all Catholic organizations worldwide for no charge. Also, homilies can be posted on a parish blog in either text, audio, or video formats, while articles, videos, and other digital content from faithful sources can be linked on parish blogs, Facebook, and Twitter accounts.

- **Evangelize:** As Cardinal O'Malley often notes, Jesus' last instruction to us, the Church, was to "Go and make disciples" of all peoples. The primary mission of the Church must also be the primary mission of those involved in the ministry of Catholic media. A key task for all of us is to ensure that our use of media doesn't "clutter" the message of Christ's saving love with "information overload." We want all our New Media applications to point visitors to Christ and to motivate them to become more engaged in parish community life.

Jeff Geerling

The Archdiocese of St. Louis uses New Media with great effect. They are active on many social-media websites, including Facebook, Twitter, and YouTube, while Archbishop Robert Carlson has his own Facebook and Twitter accounts.

Jeff Geerling (www.LifeIsAPrayer.com), who helped implement the archdiocese's web strategy, is a big reason why the archdiocese has thrived in the digital world.

"Dioceses can't afford to stay behind the curve with New Media use," Jeff explains. "Outlets like Facebook and Twitter are basically free portals to thousands — if not hundreds of thousands — of Catholics and non-Catholics alike.

"It always surprises me when an organization will spend little or no money on online development, while they spend hundreds or thousands of dollars on mail campaigns and newsletters, which are largely ignored by today's younger generations."

Despite his archdiocese's early adoption of New Media, Jeff says individuals still have mixed reactions. "Many clergy don't understand its importance or the powerful influence they could have. On the other hand, a handful of priests have been ministering in their parishes via New Media, and they have found a wider audience to whom they can proclaim the Gospel and bring people back into the fold."

Besides his work for the archdiocese, Jeff is also the founder of **Open Source Catholic** (www.OpenSourceCatholic.com), a community for Catholic techies to exchange ideas and discuss new faith-sharing technologies.

Jeff Geerling's work demonstrates how one New Media advocate can influence technology use within an entire diocese. Through Jeff, the Archdiocese of St. Louis has become a New Media model for the rest of the Church.

Ten Examples of New Media Initiatives in the Archdiocese of Boston

For the benefit of dioceses that might want to increase their New Media work but do not know the best place to start, I will profile some of our different initiatives in chronological order:

» **Cardinal Seán's Blog (CardinalSeansBlog.org)**

Six months after being elevated to the College of Cardinals in March 2006, Cardinal O'Malley returned to Rome to take possession of his titular church. He also visited San Giovanni Rotondo to celebrate the Feast Day Mass of St. Padre Pio, a fellow Capuchin. During the trip, Cardinal O'Malley wanted to share his reflections and experiences with parishioners back home through a blog. It sounded like a small, simple endeavor, but the blog's impact, both locally and globally, was enormous. Upon seeing the visitor statistics, the world's first blogging cardinal chose to continue posting on a weekly basis, hoping that the blog might also encourage other Church leaders to embrace New Media.

» **New Websites for CatholicTV.com and TheBostonPilot. com**

In late 2006 and early 2007, Cardinal O'Malley announced significant upgrades to the CatholicTV.com and TheBostonPilot. com websites. Both sites have since won numerous awards for their integration of the latest technology. CatholicTV.com continues in 2011 to be the most popular Catholic website in the world for online video programming.

» **Weekly Email From Cardinal Seán**

As part of the archdiocese's bicentennial celebration, Cardinal O'Malley instituted a weekly email in May 2008 that provides content from his blog, official press releases from the Archdiocese of Boston, links to current stories from the archdiocesan newspaper, new programs from CatholicTV®, resources for Mass and prayer, a calendar of upcoming events around the Archdiocese of Boston, and other helpful information to deepen Catholic faith life.

» **Rebranding of Archdiocesan Website (www. BostonCatholic.org)**

On St. Patrick's Day in March 2009, Cardinal O'Malley announced a new archdiocesan website. The domain name was changed from www.rcab.org to the easier-to-remember www.BostonCatholic.org. For years, the old website functioned like an online bulletin board, where we posted initiative announcements and press releases. But the new website sought to provide a "window into the soul of our Church": who we are, what we believe, how our ministries flow from the call of Christ, and our hope that others will experience the same joys we do in following Christ within the Catholic Church. We had the goal that if we were the only Catholic website that someone ever visited, there was enough information on the site (and through our direct links) to know the essentials of our Catholic faith and life. To this end, the site features a mini-catechism in addition to several links.

» **CatholicTVjr™**

In November 2009, CatholicTV® extended the power to watch its formational and entertaining programming directly on the homepages of dioceses, parishes, schools, agencies, apostolates, and even personal sites. The motivation was two-fold: to extend the reach of CatholicTV® programming and to drive up traffic and frequency on parish and school sites. CatholicTVjr™ became the world's first Catholic television widget and can be added to any website in less than three minutes by visiting www.CatholicTVjr.com.

» **The Light Is on For You (TheLightIsOnForYou.org)**

For Lent 2010, the Archdiocese of Boston launched a confession initiative following the lead of several other dioceses. The initiative's website integrated content on the Sacrament of Confession from many different Church sources. Included on the site are several videos covering the sacrament, guides explaining how to make a good confession, and embeddable logos and animated picture files which allow parishes to link graphically to the initiative's website.

» Social Media for the Archdiocese of Boston

Our Pilot New Media group was formed in July 2010 to expand the use of social media at archdiocesan and parish ministries. We have launched and extended archdiocesan social-media outposts such as Facebook.com/BostonCatholic, Twitter.com/BostonCatholic, YouTube.com/BostonCatholic, UStream.tv/user/BostonCatholic, Flickr.com/BostonCatholic, and we have helped several Church leaders implement blogs.

» Mobile Apps

In 2010, the Archdiocese of Boston launched four mobile applications for the iPhone and Android mobile devices:

- The **CatholicTV® app** provides video from the past week's Masses and Rosaries, as well as video newsbreaks, short video reflections, and CatholicTV® press releases.

- The **iCatholic app** offers users with a mobile-friendly version of the CatholicTV® *Monthly* magazine.

- The **Pilot app** provides stories on local, national, and worldwide Church news, as well as secular news from a Catholic perspective. It also provides photo slideshows from recent issues of the *Pilot*, the archdiocese's official newspaper.

- The **PilotParishFinder app** combines information from our diocesan directory with the powerful Google Maps technology to help users instantly locate churches around their current location. For each nearby parish, users can find parish information, connect instantly through phone or email, and receive driving directions from one's current location to the parish.

» Catholic New Media Celebration (CNMC)

The Archdiocese of Boston hosted SQPN.com's third annual Catholic New Media Celebration in August 2010. It was a tremendous gathering of innovators and leaders in Catholic media, and it provided inspiration to those working within the Archdiocese of Boston. If you're looking to boost your diocese's New Media efforts, consider hosting a Catholic media gathering or convention of this type.

» Catholics Come Home (CatholicsComeHomeBoston.org)

In early 2011, the Archdiocese of Boston launched the Catholics Come Home campaign, leveraging television commercials and New Media outreach to invite inactive Catholics home to the Church and to provide tools and training to assist parishes in welcoming them (see Chapter 1 for more on Catholics Come Home). A central element of this campaign was the creation of a diocesan website, www.CatholicsComeHomeBoston.org, as well as the use of our archdiocesan Facebook and Twitter accounts.

The Digital Vatican

In 1995, the Vatican became one of the earliest settlers on the digital frontier. The original **Vatican website** (www.vatican.va) was a go-to source for Church documents, history, and Catholic news. In the decade that followed, however, the website saw little change. The design remained stagnant, and outside of new papal documents, the site saw few new additions.

But with Pope Benedict XVI's emphasis on using New Media, the Vatican's online presence has rapidly changed. Today, the Vatican is firmly on the New Media bandwagon, chartering a number of innovative projects to connect with Catholics across the world.

Most impressive is the Vatican's new **Pope2You** endeavor (www.Pope2You.net), which connects Internet users to the current pontiff like never before. The Pope2You Facebook application allows thousands of users to read the pope's messages and receive "virtual postcards" through the Internet's most popular social-networking site. The Pope2You iPhone application helps you to follow the pope's travels and speeches, while the Pope2You View brings streaming live video of his weekly addresses straight to your mobile device.

The Vatican also has a heavy presence on YouTube. Their YouTube channel (www.YouTube.com/Vatican) includes over 900 videos, which have received over four million views. The videos cover the main activities of the Holy Father, his Sunday Angelus addresses, and relevant Vatican events.

Finally, the Vatican website now offers some innovative content in addition to its traditional documents. Visitors can take virtual tours of the Sistine Chapel, St. Peter's Basilica, and the Necropolis under St. Peter's, exploring these beautiful holy sites through their computer screen.

Under the leadership of Pope Benedict XVI, the Vatican has embarked on many New Media endeavors. In May 2011, Church officials invited 150 bloggers to the Vatican for a conversation about New Media. The event included a panel discussion moderated by popular Catholic blogger Rocco Palmo (http://whispersintheloggia.blogspot.com). In addition, the Vatican unveiled a new website, **www.News.va**, which utilizes many social-media tools.

Bishops and dioceses across the world should look to the Vatican for both inspiration and guidance as they similarly enter the digital frontier.

Recommendations for Dioceses and Bishops

All dioceses share the same mission of leading everyone to experience Christ's saving love. It's important that we within the Church realize that we are all on the same team. By showing what New Media projects have worked for us here in the Archdiocese of Boston, we encourage our sister dioceses to adapt any of our efforts for their own context.

With that in mind, here are some general diocesan New Media recommendations:

» 1. Establish a Dedicated Group for New Media

Cardinal O'Malley chose to reorganize our media, communication, and evangelization efforts, placing all the media organizations into one secretariat. In doing this, he separated the typically reactive public-relations ministry from the more proactive media entities. This structure has allowed our media entities to focus more on long-term initiatives and to put every media vehicle at the service of evangelization. We can deploy new innovations more rapidly now because all our media professionals work on one team.

If dioceses prefer not to create a separate secretariat, they should evaluate whether a New Media group might be more effective within a secretariat for evangelization, instead of a secretariat for communications or development.

At a minimum, I encourage dioceses to dedicate at least one full-time person to New Media. It is important that someone rises each morning with the priority of furthering the use of New Media for evangelization and communication. This task will not be fully accomplished if it is assigned to someone with an already full plate. Practically speaking, small dioceses could have one person overseeing this at first, while larger dioceses likely need a team to serve all their parishes and ministries.

The Holy Father speaks about New Media regularly and has formed the new Pontifical Council for Promoting the New Evangelization[57] to show that this outreach to the digital continent should be a top priority for the Church going forward. Dioceses should parallel the pope's emphasis.

» 2. Evaluate Your Current Strengths and Gaps in the Use of Media

Determine what media assets your diocese currently has and which ones it currently lacks (i.e., television, radio, news, print, and New Media). Then evaluate how you can improve by looking at what other dioceses are doing. Seek out those dioceses that you consider most effective and most compatible with your own situation. Find the leaders and innovators in those dioceses and request assistance and mentoring. Also, consider sharing resources within a province or episcopal region.

» 3. Create New Media Partnerships

Join up with national Catholic organizations that want to help dioceses and parishes, such as CatholicTV®, EWTN, EWTN Radio, Our Sunday Visitor, the Knights of Columbus, or one of many other Catholic groups.

» 4. Secure the Assets You Need to Engage New Media

Some dioceses might be able to accomplish this through reallocating their budget. Most might need to fund-raise to grow their use of New Media. Our experience in the Archdiocese of Boston has shown that one of the most preferred reasons for giving to the Church here is to hand on our faith to young Catholics. Just as so many benefactors have stepped forward to support our New Media efforts here in Boston, I'm confident that Catholics in your diocese will support this work in your area.

» 5. Begin With a Few Initiatives at the Diocesan Level

Model excellence in the use of social media and blogs at the diocesan level to demonstrate to parishes, schools, and other agencies how it can be accomplished. The examples of what you are able to accomplish can help your fund-raising efforts, which will then help acquire New Media staff to assist all the parishes, schools, and agencies of your diocese.

» 6. Commit to Helping Parishes, Schools, and Agencies Within Your Diocesan New Media Group

Working together in New Media could be a great way to bring parishes and central ministries of a diocese more closely together. So much digital content can be shared among the various organizations within a diocese that it makes sense to have someone coordinating this sharing. The 7E's that were discussed earlier can provide a good road map for encouraging greater New Media adoption in your diocese.

» 7. Sponsor and Host Gatherings of New Media Enthusiasts

The Holy Father hasn't called us to evangelize the digital continent all by ourselves — it is the work of the entire Church. This is best accomplished when we all know one another, share ideas, support one another, and learn from one another's successes and failures. Hosting an annual convocation and awards celebration in your diocese can inspire other Catholics to step forward to help construct New Media platforms to support evangelization, formation, and information sharing. It can also be a great way to line up financial support for your own New Media endeavors. The Catholic New Media Celebration by SQPN is a template for a great New Media gathering.

» 8. Make Your Media Operations Multilingual

Within the Archdiocese of Boston, this is the next significant phase of our media-growth plan. For a large percentage of younger Catholics in the United States, English is not their first language. We want to reach them in a language that will help them most appreciate the person of Jesus Christ and the treasure of his Catholic Church. After we establish our presence in English, we will then seek out the best ways to deploy in other languages and cultures.

Conclusion

Pope Benedict XVI has asked all those with experience or interest in New Media to embrace the task of evangelization at this critical time for the Church. Along with the Archdiocese of Boston, I encourage you to take up this holy and sacred task. And I ask God's blessings on your initiatives in New Media and request your prayers for our efforts in the Archdiocese of Boston.

Scot Landry is the secretary for Catholic media of the Roman Catholic Archdiocese of Boston. He oversees the archdiocese's media entities, including CatholicTV, the *Pilot* newspaper, Pilot Bulletins, Pilot Printing, Pilot New Media, and the Radio Apostolate. As a member of the steering committee of Cardinal Seán O'Malley's cabinet, he also is heavily involved in strategic planning, resource allocation, and implementation of major initiatives. Scot lives in Belmont, Massachusetts, with his wife and three children.

Chapter 8
// High-Tech Community: New Media in the Parish //
Matt Warner

New Media. These can be scary words for parishioners and their leaders. Part of this discomfort stems from the usual fear of the *new*, the unknown. Another part arises from the "untamed" stereotype that is often associated with the Internet: "Who will moderate comments? What if people use it inappropriately? We've been communicating just fine up until now — it's not worth the risks!"

But the truth is this: Poor communication is one of the most common problems within parish communities. And as the Vatican reminds us, if New Media is used wisely, it can become "a valid and effective instrument for authentic and profound evangelization and communion."[58]

In the parish days of old, traditional forms of communication were perfectly adequate. People lived in villages that revolved around parish life. Their social lives, spiritual lives, and even their jobs were spent in the same community. Today, however, people are pulled in thousands of directions — and too many of these directions are away from the Church. To engage our parishioners, we must reach them where they already are and how they're already communicating.

This doesn't mean sacrificing a greater good. It means embracing a greater opportunity. Never before have we had the means to communicate on the level that modern technology allows. As Pope Benedict says, "New communications media, if adequately understood and exploited, can offer priests and all pastoral care workers a wealth of data which was difficult to access before, and facilitate forms of collaboration and increased communion that were previously unthinkable."[59]

Here's a familiar scenario: Many parishes use Mass announcements and bulletins as their primary means of communicating. The problem? Too many announcements can interrupt the liturgy — and fall on deaf ears of tuned-out parishioners. And expensive paper bulletins (which are often outdated and hard to navigate) end up under the seat in the car or as paper airplanes for the kids. Neither form of communication engages parishioners with the targeted, up-to-the-minute information they're used to. With these underwhelming communication vehicles, we spend more time begging for attention — and less time building thriving relationships that fuel the life of the parish.

Instead of holding parishioners hostage during the liturgy with an onslaught of announcements (because it's the only time you have their ear), imagine being in solid contact with them *throughout* the week.

Instead of only getting to know parishioners who stick around for doughnuts, imagine connecting with everyone who walks through your parish doors (and with some who don't even do that).

Instead of only relying on a small parish council for feedback, imagine giving *all* of your parishioners an easy, safe forum to share their voice. After all, New Media is not just about being a better communicator; it's also about being a better listener. By embracing these new forms of communication, we can reach our flocks — even when they're not in the pews.

And New Media is not just about remote communication. It's also about enhancing how we present and share the faith *within* the parish building. This includes using high-quality video and audio to help teach classes and enhance presentations, or utilizing compelling forms of technology to entertain and emcee at community functions. It also means allowing parishioners to access material online and to continue the conversation when they get home.

Finally, we can't forget about better business productivity. Instead of a small, over-burdened staff trying to deal with cumbersome paperwork and time-consuming bookkeeping using out-of-date software, New Media provides an operational staff with ways to manage their parish more efficiently and effectively than ever before.

So often we scoff at these tools because we believe they will compete with what's *most* important. But the irony is, used correctly, these God-given communication tools actually enhance what's most important.

To do that, we need to first understand five New Media rules of parish communication.

//

RULE #1: THE PARISHIONER IS IN CONTROL

We live in an age of permission-based communication. People are tired of junk mail. They hate spam. And they *really* hate unsolicited salespeople. We fast-forward through commercials. We ignore billboards. We turn off as soon as we think somebody is trying to sell us something — or force us to listen to something we didn't sign up for. If we really want to reach people, we need to do so *the way they want to listen* — and usually only if they want to listen in the first place.

Eighty percent of Americans (and presumably, churchgoers too) use some form of social media.[60] Sixty-eight percent of churchgoers want to connect with their church via social media.[61] Most parishioners regularly use email and text messaging to communicate in their personal and professional lives. But most of them do not read their parish bulletin. Most of them are not officially registered at their parish. Many are not inspired about their parish. And sadly, most do not think about their parish in between Sundays.

By allowing parishioners to control their means of communication, it is more likely that they will stay connected and engaged throughout the week.

> *"Priests stand at the threshold of a new era: as new technologies create deeper forms of relationship across greater distances, they are called to respond pastorally by putting the media ever more effectively at the service of the Word....*
>
> *"Priests are thus challenged to proclaim the Gospel by employing the latest generation of audiovisual resources (images, videos, animated features, blogs, websites) which, alongside traditional means, can open up broad new vistas for dialogue, evangelization and catechesis."[62]*
>
> — POPE BENEDICT XVI, MESSAGE FOR THE 44TH WORLD COMMUNICATIONS DAY (2010)

RULE #2: YOUR WEBSITE MATTERS

In this age, your parish website is often the first (and sometimes last) impression a visitor has of your parish. For simply practical purposes, if somebody can't find your website, you don't exist. On top of that, if your website looks terrible, it's a poor reflection upon how well your parish is run and how seriously it takes its mission. Right or wrong, that's how people are judging your parish right now. Your website matters.

Unfortunately, many parish websites are subpar and are committing some very deadly sins of web design. They are littered with auto-playing music, cheesy animated graphics, flashing text, visitor counters, and ridiculous menus all pointing to outdated information that you can barely read over the poorly chosen background image. Even many "good" ones are hard to navigate and are underwhelming.

We must do better. Think of your website as your New Media home base. It needs to be high quality, easy to use, and filled with meaningful content. Most of all, it needs to connect the visitors to what they are searching for. You can't just have a website. It must serve a purpose.

So, what is this purpose? It's twofold:

1. To help visitors *easily* find the information they're looking for.

2. To connect with parishioners by:

    a. Getting them subscribed to a mailing list.

    b. Capturing their email, phone number, and other registration information.

    c. Engaging them on Facebook, Twitter, or elsewhere.

    d. All of the above.

Don't know where to start? Here's some advice to help your parish website serve a purpose:

- Get help from someone who *really* knows about building professional websites (not just the first volunteer standing around who likes HTML).

- Spend more money on your website than you do on doughnuts.

- Spend much less money on it than you would a new car.

- When somebody first visits your website, he or she should know who you are and what you're about within four seconds.

- Make sure multiple leaders in your parish — preferably every ministry leader — can update their part of the website. Otherwise, you end up with inefficient bottlenecks for new information. (Check out www.eCatholicChurches.com for one such solution.)

- Less is more. Having *too* much information can make it harder for visitors to find what they actually need.

- Think about five to seven main reasons somebody visits your website, then build your front page and navigation system around that.

- Have Mass times, confession times, phone number(s), and your address somewhere easy to find (these are four of the five to seven main reasons somebody visits your website).

- Offer quick and easy online registration and tithing (these are two more main reasons).

- Make it easy to browse and connect with different parish ministries.

- Offer online event registration.

- Choose a simple, elegant color palette.

- Have something that reaches out to fallen-away Catholics who may stop by. Check out www.CatholicsComeHome. org (see sidebar in Chapter 1) for ideas and resources to link to.

- Tell the story of your parish — the history, symbolism, art, architecture, and the meaning behind it all. For a bonus, do this using video.

- Use, embed, and link to a lot of the wonderful Catholic New Media resources already online that will help parishioners in their faith journey.

RULE #3: REACH PEOPLE WHERE THEY ALREADY ARE

Though websites matter, most savvy Internet users do not regularly check websites for information anymore. This means your parish website must do more than just post information — it must push information out to people the way they want to receive it. So it's very important that when they do happen to visit your website, you use that opportunity to connect with them in order to continue the relationship. Here are some ways to do that:

» Email

Email is a New Media staple. Almost everyone uses it — and anyone with Internet access can create an email address for free in a few minutes. However, there are some considerations to being a safe and effective emailer:

- Use a professional emailing service that not only keeps your ISP from labeling you a spammer but that also provides some basic features (like an unsubscribe button, which you legally need to have in your outgoing email). A professional service will also help you send fancy emails, manage invalid or expired addresses, and track all kinds of other potentially helpful statistics in your email communication. This type of service is relatively cheap and pays for itself due to the reduced need for expensive paper mail-outs.

- As I stated before, have a link on your website for visitors to easily subscribe via email to your parish mailings *and* specific ministry distribution lists.

- Be prudent. If you send people too much unnecessary email, they will unsubscribe, and you'll have lost them.

- If some parishioners don't have an email address, provide a free class at your parish to teach them and get them set up. Most public libraries offer free Internet access too.

» Text Messaging

Sixty-three percent of Americans use text messaging (this includes people from all ages, races, and income levels).[63] And that number is quickly increasing every year. This means that the ability for parishioners to pull out their phones and subscribe to a text-message mailing list is very powerful. Not only is it easier to sign up for information via text, but it's also the easiest way to receive important reminders and notifications.

Here are some texting tips:

- Start investing now. Bulk-texting may currently be a bit expensive for some, but it is getting cheaper and cheaper every day.

- Once you are able, offer short codes for people to immediately subscribe via text message to events, ministries, and mailing lists.

- Be conscious of sending out bulk text messages late at night or early in the morning unnecessarily.

- Also be aware that some parishioners' phone plans will charge them for each text message they receive. Make sure they have clear options on how to opt out of such messages if they need to.

» Blogging, Podcasting, and Video

Blogs, podcasts, and videos are the perfect way to spice up your website and social-media presence. Through these mediums, you can easily post the latest parish news, thoughts from the pastor, homilies, and any audio or video of interest. They are wonderful mediums for expressing creativity as well.

Here are some considerations when using these communication channels:

- If a blog is not built into your website already, it's fairly easy to add a free or cheap blog to it (try WordPress.com or Blogger.com).

- Post regularly on your blog and solicit high-quality contributions from staff and select parishioners. It will encourage engagement within the parish and will make sure there is always fresh content on the website.

- Record talks and homilies given at your parish (audio and/ or video), and offer them on your website for parishioners (and others) to enjoy from home.

- Fun idea: Launch a video contest where parishioners produce a fun video explaining something neat about your parish. Put it all on the website for others to learn from.

- Get in touch with your creative side ... and with your creative parishioners.

- Have parish leaders record a short intro video for their ministries and post it on the website.

- Quality is not everything, but it's worth something. If it's an official parish video, make it high quality. Remember, it is all a reflection of your parish and the Church.

- Be patient. You may not be professionals at it on your first try. But focus on improving and getting better with each go-round. There are lots of free resources out there to help.

Angela Santana

The Church includes a number of Catholics who are interested in technology, but **Angela Santana** (www.twitter.com/ InspiredAngela) is one of New Media's strongest advocates. Angela graduated from St. Mary's University, where she earned a B.A. in English communication arts, concentrating in marketing and theology. As the culmination of her studies, Angela wrote an honors thesis titled *New Media, New Evangelization*, which introduced ways that Catholics can best use New Media tools.

After college, Angela particularly focused on New Media use at the parish level. In her home diocese of San Antonio, Texas, she's led multiple New Media workshops with parish and diocesan leaders. Angela covers topics like podcasting and videocasting, and has also given a presentation on "Reaching Individuals in a Social-Media Age." To help other New Media pioneers, Angela has made all of her presentations available online for free (www.SlideShare.net/InspiredAngela).

But Angela's work has taken her far beyond the Lone Star State. As part of the Pilgrim Center of Hope, a Catholic evangelization ministry, she embarked on a New Media pilgrimage to the Holy Land. Followers of the Pilgrim Center blog were able to journey alongside Angela, experiencing the sights and sounds of biblical lands through blog posts, Facebook photo galleries, and YouTube videocasts. They shared in the wonder of Petra, the somberness of the Garden of Gethsemane, and the celebration of Bethlehem.

Finally, in addition to being the ministry coordinator for the Pilgrim Center of Hope, Angela runs her own apostolate called **Inspired Ministry Solutions** (www.Facebook.com/InspiredMinistrySolutions). Through her apostolate, Angela provides New Media help for Catholic ministries and people with all levels of digital experience.

As parishes embrace these tools, each would do well to find someone like Angela to spearhead the charge.

» Facebook, Twitter, and Other Social Networks

Sorting through endless social-networking websites is quite the task. In fact, by the time this is published, there will probably be something new. But there are a couple, like Facebook and Twitter, that (for now, at least) have established themselves as social-media bread and butter. So they're a good place to start.

Most often, social media are not as direct as email and text messaging, but it is increasingly important that you have a presence there. Otherwise, people may start to think you don't exist. Besides, the benefits are potentially huge.

Here are a few tips for navigating the social net:

- Personally use it. *You* need to understand, first-hand, how it works and how it can benefit your parish. Get help if you need it.

- Be an example online of how we can use social media in a holy way by building quality relationships and maintaining healthy boundaries.

- Create a Facebook page (*not* a personal profile) for your parish (see the Appendix to learn the difference between the two). Invite parishioners to follow along.

- Post all of the latest content from your website or blog on your Facebook page as it is created. There are even some tools that will do this automatically for you.

- Start conversations. Post articles and links of interest. Do your best to keep it moderated and charitable.

- Let go. Yes, somebody may eventually say something rude or inappropriate. You can't control it any more or less on your Facebook page than if you were all sitting around a table in the parish hall. Warn troublemakers. Block repeat offenders. Most importantly, move forward. Don't let a few knuckleheads ruin it for everyone else.

- Create a Twitter profile for your parish, and start following other parishes in your diocese too. To start, you can share all of the things on Twitter that you share on your Facebook page. Over time, you'll get a better feel for the various ways you can use Twitter.

- Add yourself to www.TweetCatholic.com, where you'll find some other great Catholic tweeters too.

- Try to update Facebook and Twitter with at least something new every day.

- Finally, listen more than you talk.

» flockNote

I have to mention flockNote.com — and not just because it's been my passion and life's work for the past couple of years, but because it was made to accomplish *exactly* what I've been talking about here. It's specifically made for Catholic parishes and is a perfect example of what we can do when we uniquely apply New Media to the work of the Church. Here's the gist.

Imagine letting all of your parishioners pull out their cell phones after Mass on Sunday and asking them to text-message a keyword and their email address to a particular five-digit phone number. Immediately, you capture their phone number and their email address and then subscribe them to a specified distribution list. An automatic email is sent to them, asking them to confirm their email address and to complete their registration.

They complete their registration in just minutes — and now you've captured some additional and totally customizable information about them. Immediately after they submit that info, they are presented a list of all of the ministries you offer in your parish. They can quickly subscribe to anything and everything you have to offer and be immediately plugged in.

Better yet, when they subscribe to each list, they can choose to be notified via email, text message, Twitter, or any combination thereof. They can also follow along via Facebook and RSS if they'd like. And for those people who don't have cell phones or email, you can have the system make an automated phone call to them each time new information is posted to a particular list.

People can also register on your parish website via an easily embedded flockNote form. And if you have an existing email list, you can simply import that list directly into flockNote and start using it. More than just another communication tool, flockNote can handle your online parish registration, bulk emailing, bulk text-messaging, event registration and RSVPs, polling, scheduled notes, small-group discussions, custom electronic parish bulletins, and much more. You can learn more at flockNote.com (and see Chapter 3 for an example of flockNote in action at St. Mary's Catholic Center in Texas).

Rule #4: Don't Give Up

I'd be lying if I said this was all easy. Implementing a new communication system has its challenges — yet they're worth overcoming.

No matter how loudly people complain about change, keep in mind that they rarely represent the silent majority. Don't let a vocal minority ruin good things for everyone else.

Speaking of complaining, let's not overlook ourselves. If we are one of the decision makers at our parish, we should be careful to make sure that we are not the reason the parish is lagging behind in its communication efforts. It's easy to let our own personal preferences, biases, experiences, or technological disabilities be what keeps our parish from being the best it can be. Know your weaknesses — that's half the battle — and then compensate for them.

Taking the step toward better communication may also require some investment in training and maintenance. But it's an inevitable investment well worth making.

Mostly, don't be afraid.

We can't shrink in fear at what kinds of dangers lurk behind our overly secure firewalls. Sure, there are risks to using New Media (as there are with everything in life). But there are also risks to the status quo — and much greater risks at that.

Parish Websites and Social-Media Guidance

A recent survey of church communication directors revealed a strong desire to engage social media — only 2 percent said they personally avoid the technology — but the large majority said they needed help with this engagement.[64] Thankfully, many Catholics have been utilizing these New Media tools for a while and openly share their expertise online.

Carson Weber (www.CarsonWeber.org), the associate director for New Media evangelization in the Diocese of Sacramento in California, realized that while almost every parish in his diocese had a website, most weren't sure how best to use it. In response, Carson gave a presentation to diocesan clergy and parish staff titled *The Parish Website — An Essential Tool for Ministry,* which he has made available for free online (www. Diocese-Sacramento.org/website). In his presentation, Carson covers the essential features that every parish website should have, while also touching on the design, navigation, and content of good parish sites.

"What the parish bulletin was 20 years ago, the parish website will dwarf in the immediate years to come," Carson says. "While once a nice perk, this relatively new communication medium is becoming a necessity as our communication evolves from print to digital. The parish website will soon be the prerequisite of effective parish communication, and we would be fools to ignore its necessity."

Jonathan Sullivan (www.JonathanFSullivan.com), the director of catechetical ministries for the Diocese of Springfield in Illinois, is another Catholic answering the request for New Media help. Focusing especially on the use of New Media in catechesis, Jonathan has a presentation titled *Catechizing Digital Natives* (www.JonathanFSullivan. com/-DigitalNatives), which teaches catechists how to speak the online vernacular and become familiar with digital generations. For parish leaders wanting to learn more about Facebook and other social-networking tools, Jonathan has two other free presentations: *Reaching Parishioners with Facebook* (www.JonathanFSullivan.com) and *Social Networking — A Primer* (www.JonathanFSullivan.com/-SocialNetworking).

"In every age, the Church has used the tools at her disposal for passing on the faith and calling people to become disciples of Christ," Jonathan explains. "By establishing Facebook pages, posting online videos, sending out text messages, and responding to tweets, parishes can connect with the faithful and the wider culture in a way the great missionaries could only dream of. We just need the courage to try."

RULE #5: ENGAGE THEIR HEARTS FIRST

Many parish leaders wonder why they have such trouble getting contact information and participation from their parishioners. I see three reasons why this is.

The first, and perhaps most important, reason is that parishioners aren't inspired. New Media is just that — a medium. It's not all that inspiring by itself. What is inspiring is the truth and love it can communicate. When someone joins your parish, they're not just joining a social network; they're encountering a sacramental and active means of participating in the life of something much bigger — the one, holy, Catholic, and apostolic Church. Now that's something to get inspired about.

Perhaps Pope Benedict says it best. When speaking of New Media he says:

> If your mission is to be truly effective — if the words you proclaim are to touch hearts, engage people's freedom and change their lives — you must draw them into an encounter with persons and communities who witness to the grace of Christ by their faith and their lives.[65]

The second reason parishioners hesitate to get plugged in is that many parishes are in maintenance mode. They aren't growing. They aren't run professionally. They aren't forward-looking. They've lost their missionary spirit.

People like to be connected to things that are going somewhere. And by not using the latest communication technologies, parishes send a message to visitors that says, "Hey, we can't even be bothered to make the effort to speak your language." Nobody gets excited to be a part of something like that.

The third reason for disengagement is simple: a lack of trust. It's quite sad, but true. Too many parishes have abused their parishioners' trust. They've held us hostage at Mass and forced us to listen to endless announcements that apply to a small fraction of the community. They blast you with emails you can't unsubscribe from that clutter your inbox with information that doesn't pertain to you.

To truly connect in a meaningful, inspiring way, we must change the ways we connect with our parishioners. Speak to their hearts, earn their trust, and communicate on their terms.

//

A Few More Recommendations

- Form a qualified Digital Communications Council. Recruit the experts sitting in your pews and come up with a one-year, quantifiable, and measureable plan to implement a formal communication strategy.

- Empower the Digital Communications Council to actually do something, including giving them a serious budget. Again, give them more than you spend on doughnuts.

- Do not overpay for New Media services. It pains me to hear how much money some parishes spend on relatively inexpensive things. Educate yourselves before you spend.

- If possible, hire somebody to manage your New Media efforts. Think of it as an investment. Hire a well-qualified person for a year and see how much participation and tithing go up.

- Use this communication effort as an opportunity to reach out and involve a lot of the young people in the parish who are experts on this topic. Pastoral leadership is extremely important. All leadership should be on board with your communication plan, and active participation by the pastor and other priests is extremely beneficial.

- Pray, hope, and don't worry. And most of all, have fun!

Final Thoughts

Change is scary but inevitable. What's scarier is losing the hearts and minds of our parishioners. The Catholic Church has one thing that will never change: the fullness of Truth and grace given by Jesus Christ. And the best way to communicate that Truth is in a way people will listen and relate. This is the power of New Media.

Matt Warner is a Catholic husband, father, tweeter, blogger, and entrepreneur. In 2008, Matt left his engineering career to focus full time on New Media and the Catholic faith. He is the founder of flockNote.com and his personal blog, FallibleBlogma.com. Matt is also a featured blogger for the *National Catholic Register* at NCRegister.com. In his free time, he can be found changing diapers and building Lego empires. Matt has a B.S. in electrical engineering from Texas A&M and an M.B.A. in entrepreneurship. He and his family hang their hats in Texas.

CHAPTER 9

// That They May Be One: Cultivating Online Community //
Lisa M. Hendey

When I launched **CatholicMom.com** in 2000, my motivation was largely to find support in my vocation as a wife and mother. At the time, my husband, Greg, and I were deeply entrenched in our family's little Domestic Church, but Greg had not yet entered the Catholic Church. Feeling the full weight of my duty to raise my two sons in the faith was a burden I didn't fully know how to bear on my own, so I went looking online for community, for help to carry out this most important of my mothering duties.

An Online Community Blossoms

In those days, the extent of my Internet experience was the ability to check my email on AOL. A volunteer stint as the Catholic school webmaster, an early version of Microsoft FrontPage, and a slew of *"Dummies"* books constituted the training for what I was convinced would be a passing hobby. A preliminary search of the Internet for the term "Catholic Mom" in those days, when even Google was just getting off the ground, yielded minimal results.

Somehow, despite my scant technical knowledge, and fully aware of the limitations of my own abilities, I registered the domain CatholicMom.com and began to dream big about creating a space that would "Celebrate Catholic Motherhood." These many years later, my aspirations continue to outpace my technical expertise. But so many tools that evolved over the years have helped my hobby blossom into a vocation I share with the over 100 contributors, who make CatholicMom.com a virtual home for so many. Last year, we welcomed visitors from over 190 countries and territories who came to us in search of that same connection I sought in the late 1990s — a place to learn about, to share, to grow in, and most importantly to celebrate the treasures of our Catholic faith.

These years have given me a front row seat for many of the challenges our Church has faced. And they have blessed me with a community of Catholic friends which literally spans the globe. In an age when the word "friend" sometimes bears shallow meaning, I've been supported by an ever-widening circle of men, women, teens and children, laity, ordained and religious, who have taught me daily what the four Marks of the Church — "one, holy, Catholic, and apostolic" — truly mean.

Time and time again, I have seen online relationships blossom into "real world" friendships. It is this sense of community, of being a part of a larger whole, that has come to define the ever-growing Church online for so many of us who supplement our local parish commitments and involvement with a worldwide role in the body of Christ.

> *"In this light, reflecting on the significance of the new technologies, it is important to focus not just on their undoubted capacity to foster contact between people, but on the quality of the content that is put into circulation using these means. I would encourage all people of good will who are active in the emerging environment of digital communication to commit themselves to promoting a culture of respect, dialogue and friendship."*[66]
> — POPE BENEDICT XVI, MESSAGE FOR THE 43RD WORLD COMMUNICATIONS DAY (2009)

> *"It is important, therefore, that the Christian community think of very practical ways of helping those who first make contact through the Internet to move from the virtual world of cyberspace to the real world of Christian community."*[67]
> — BLESSED JOHN PAUL II, MESSAGE FOR THE 36TH WORLD COMMUNICATIONS DAY (2002)

Online Communities and Catholic Life

In January of 2010, Pope Benedict XVI called on the universal Church to pray for a timely general intercession: "That young people may learn to use modern means of social communication for their personal growth and to better prepare themselves to serve society."[68]

While his comments may have been directed toward our youth, these two goals for using modern means of communication — for personal growth and to better prepare ourselves to serve society — continue to underscore the importance of fostering community in our online endeavors. This intercession followed on the heels of another wonderful message from Pope Benedict XVI, on the occasion of the 43rd World Communications Day:

> When we find ourselves drawn towards other people, when we want to know more about them and make ourselves known to them, we are responding to God's call — a call that is imprinted in our nature as beings created in the image and likeness of God, the God of communication and communion.[69]

It is this deeper desire to know one another, to form true community online, that has transformed the Internet from a static source of information into a living, breathing entity that continues to transform the way in which we communicate with one another, not only on a larger societal level but even within the intimacy of our own families. And for our Church as she endeavors to embrace the digital revolution, for individual parish communities that hope to harness the power of New Media, and for individuals looking to share their faith online, a primary goal in our efforts should be to truly build up dialogue through our work.

No longer is it good enough to simply post a parish bulletin or slap up an article on Lenten practices. What this technology has unleashed, and what our Holy Father is calling us to, is a more conversational tone that not only prompts but actually encourages two-way communication about the issues and teachings we hold most dear — conversation that respects those involved in the dialogue and that is always true to the teachings of the Church. Pope Benedict says that:

> In the final analysis, the truth of Christ is the full and authentic response to that human desire for relationship, communion and meaning which is reflected in the immense popularity of social networks. Believers who bear witness to their most profound convictions greatly help prevent the web from becoming an instrument which depersonalizes people, attempts to manipulate them emotionally or allows those who are powerful to monopolize the opinions of others. On the contrary, believers encourage everyone to keep alive the eternal human questions which testify to our desire for transcendence and our longing for authentic forms of life, truly worthy of being lived. It is precisely this uniquely human spiritual yearning which inspires our quest for truth and for communion and which impels us to communicate with integrity and honesty.[70]

Blogging Builds Community

Cognizant of this deeper desire for communion, and armed with today's latest tools, we have the ability to fuel true conversation in our online endeavors. Perhaps one of the greatest examples of online community is happening today in the world of blogging.

The term "mommy blogger" now defines an ever-growing community of women who have taken to the Internet in the way our mothers used to gather for coffee in one another's kitchens. But this conversation is not just about reviewing products or sharing potty-training tips. Today's mothers have found support, strength, and true community online in both the world of social networking and in the blogosphere. New generations of parents are turning to one another online for answers to everything from medical woes in infants to how to deal with the turbulent teenager.

A mom who blogs may share her take on how to get a "terrible two" to sit through Mass, but more often she'll start the conversation with a blog post and then invite her readers — her community — to offer the real teaching through their responses in the comment box. Where previous generations of moms gathered for Rosary groups or play dates at the Catholic school playground, today's mothers tend to supplement their "real world" friendships with the vibrant communities that have cropped up around the Internet in places like CatholicMom. com or FaithAndFamilyLive.com. The resulting relationships and conversations build mutual respect, true dialogue, and lasting friendship.

These days, it's not unusual for me to have the great joy of a face-to-face meeting with a Facebook friend or to break bread with a blog reader or podcast listener when I travel. The ability to extend the time we share in cyberspace into more lasting friendships is one of the greatest joys of being part of the Church online.

Faith and Family Connect

While New Media tools can bring together people already living in proximity, they are most powerfully used when gathering people who are far apart. Whether connecting Catholic activists in Florida with others in Oregon or gathering religious sisters from multiple continents, New Media stimulates community in ways that would be impossible in an offline world.

Faith and Family Connect (www.Connect. FaithAndFamilyLive.com) — part of the larger Faith and

Family Live — exemplifies this dynamic of communal gathering. The site is a self-described go-to destination for Catholic women "seeking information, inspiration, resources, and encouragement as they embrace their vocations to marriage and motherhood." Women log on to the website to learn, share, and grow alongside fellow women from across the world.

The Faith and Family Connect community is cultivated through many ways: a blog with multiple daily entries, an online photo gallery, an active discussion forum, a "groups" feature which connects women of similar locations and interests, and plenty of dialogue through the comment boxes scattered throughout the website. For those seeking a more immediate connection, the site also has a chat room to host conversation among Catholic women.

Faith and Family Connect has become a digital front porch for thousands of Catholics, a beautiful example of New Media's communal power in action.

Faith Sharing by Podcast

This desire for increased community has also spurred the popularity of online media forms such as podcasting, video sharing, and social networking. Our desire to know one another more deeply has encouraged many of us to take our passions to the airwaves in new ways.

My weekly "Catholic Moments" podcast is just one example of this — with simple recording software and an inexpensive web-hosting plan, I can share my enthusiasm for Catholic literature and music, or simply highlight the work of ordinary Catholics who are sharing their faith in extraordinary ways.

A housewife from Fresno can become a New Media evangelist, but the greatest capacity of tools like podcasting comes from the community that develops around this form of

New Media. The consumers are invited to become part of — and indeed to truly shape — the content and the conversation. The community's feedback becomes as vital to the program as the host herself. The shared experience and a common desire to grow in faith and to lift one another to heaven are tangible signs of the Holy Spirit at work in these new forms of media. While I may never be the next "Barbara Walters," my weekly podcast enables me to highlight my faith in new and creative ways, proclaiming the Good News and making new friends along the way.

Finding a Balance

One constant challenge for those of us who have ventured online to share and learn about our faith is the balancing act between our digital evangelization efforts and our "real world" responsibilities and relationships. We need to constantly guard ourselves against the lure of online status-seeking or neglect of our family. Pope Benedict XVI wisely commented on this in his message for the 45th World Communications Day:

> Entering cyberspace can be a sign of an authentic search for personal encounters with others, provided that attention is paid to avoiding dangers such as enclosing oneself in a sort of parallel existence, or excessive exposure to the virtual world. In the search for sharing, for "friends," there is the challenge to be authentic and faithful, and not give in to the illusion of constructing an artificial public profile for oneself.[71]

Communicating With Care

In our efforts to build and to be a positive part of online communities, we must always operate with balance. We're also called to remember that our online communities may well include non-Catholic friends and contacts. For those who do not share our beliefs, our posts, status updates, and tweets may often be the only contact that they have with our Church. When we air our dirty laundry online or engage in divisive rhetoric, we give them ammunition to perpetuate their stereotypes about us. However, when we proclaim our faith with joy, we send a message about the truths we hold dear, and we inspire others to learn more about the cause for our happiness.

A wise media friend told me years ago, "Don't say anything online that you wouldn't say to someone's face." In building and fostering online communities, we must always remember that our goal is real relationships, based in trust and mutual respect. My personal experience has taught me that our world is increasingly interconnected, thanks to today's technology, which often produces a "six degrees of separation" phenomenon that results in online contacts becoming "real world" friends.

I prefer to frequent online environments that foster communities which build up friendship rather than point out shortcomings. This is the type of environment I've strived to develop on CatholicMom.com — a place of mutual respect and of tangible camaraderie.

Catholic New Media Community

Beginning to use New Media can seem intimidating. With a wide selection of technologies and a rapidly changing digital world, determining where to start is hard. But it's important to realize that you are not alone.

Thankfully, a growing community of Catholic New Media experts has blossomed online. These men and women — both clergy and laypeople, young and old — provide support, encouragement, and assistance with many New Media tools. Need help with your new blog? Wondering how you can best use Facebook or Twitter? Trying to decide what equipment you need for your podcast? Plenty of Catholics across the Internet are ready to help.

For guidance and advice, begin at the website for this book, **Church and New Media** (ChurchAndNewMedia.

com). From there, look to the **Catholic Media Guild** (www.
CatholicMediaGuild.com), **Catholic Tech Talk** (www.
CatholicTechTalk.com), or search Twitter using the **Catholic
New Media** hashtag (#cathmedia).[72] For more advanced
users, **Open Source Catholic** (www.OpenSourceCatholic.
com) is another great place to find help from experienced
Catholic techies.

If you need inspiration rather than technical advice, turn
each year to the **Catholic New Media awards** (www.
CatholicNewMediaAwards.com) or the **About.com Catholic
Readers' Choice awards** (www.Catholicism.About.com) to
discover the best websites, blogs, podcasts, and videocasts
in many different categories. The annual **Catholic Media
Promotion Day** (www.PromoteCatholicism.com) provides
another great source for stellar Catholic media.

Besides advice and inspiration, the Catholic New Media
community is a great place to meet others with similar gifts
and interests.

"The Catholic New Media community can be an incredibly
encouraging place to be," says Catholic radio host and
podcaster **Lino Rulli** (www.LinoRulli.com). "The strength of
communities formed through Catholic New Media is that
like-minded Catholics can talk about what's going on in their
parish, their diocese, or the Church at large. The community
that some of us may lack in our own parish can find a virtual
community. And that's an amazing thing."

Not settling for online-only relationships, many Catholic
New Media pioneers have begun joining up across the
country. Three annual conferences — the Catholic New Media
Celebration, CatholiCon, and Interactive Connections — bring
together people interested in New Media and the Church,
offering training, exhibitions, and time to socialize with online
friends. Through these gatherings, relationships cultivated in
the digital world lead to in-person friendships, just as Pope
Benedict XVI has repeatedly encouraged.

Fostering Conversation and Friendship

Online community does not build itself. In order for true dialogue to develop, there are necessary ingredients. Obviously, the technology itself must invite and facilitate conversation. These days, content-management systems make it easy and affordable to build websites that not only look great but which promote user participation. But beyond the technological requirements, our online environments themselves must open the door to discussion.

Our blog posts must be written with an eye toward involving and valuing the readers' experience and wisdom. Our facilitation of comment-box conversations must send the signal that we welcome input, but that we also require respect and truth. When we, as bloggers or even as masters of our own social-networking pages, permit comment-box conversation that degrades into enraged dialogue, we are disrespecting our communities. A blogger who is concerned with fostering friendship online should spend as much time and energy focusing on the comboxes as she does on her posts. In this brave new world of social communications, to do anything less is to dissuade the true friendship, respect, and dialogue our Church has called us to create.

The following practical pointers sum up my advice for fostering communities online:

- Use content-management-system (CMS) software that facilitates commenting.

- Create and publish a comment-moderation policy that allows for dialogue but provides consequences for abuse.

- Implement social-networking plug-ins to bring the social-networking experience to your blog.

- Write to incite conversation. Close posts with open-ended questions, and invite community members to share their experiences and perspectives.

- Experiment with podcasting, streaming video, and chat to bring New Media outlets into your community.

- Carefully study the most recent World Communications Day messages from Pope Benedict XVI for a faith-filled perspective on fostering true community.

As technological advances continue to emerge, the truth of our faith and its great beauty for our lives remain consistent. Just as the early Church Fathers employed every means at their disposal to build up and edify the body of Christ, you and I have the same opportunity today to pray for one another and to build a Church that is nurtured and strengthened by the gift of friendship in Christ.

Lisa M. Hendey is the founder and editor of **CatholicMom. com** and the author of *The Handbook for Catholic Moms.* Lisa hosts the weekly "Catholic Moments Podcast" and the "Catholic Mom" television segments on KNXT-TV. She writes for Faith and Family Live, and her articles have appeared in the *National Catholic Register, Our Sunday Visitor,* and many other websites and periodicals. Lisa speaks nationally on faith, family, and Catholic New Media topics. She resides in the Diocese of Fresno with her husband, Greg, and teenage sons, Eric and Adam.

// Part Four //

To the Ends of the Earth: New Media and the Common Good

CHAPTER 10
// Changing the World: New Media Activism //
Thomas Peters

> *"The fate of a society always depends on its creative minorities…. Christian believers should look upon themselves as just such a creative minority."*[73]
>
> — POPE BENEDICT XVI, QUOTING BRITISH HISTORIAN ARNOLD TOYNBEE

The Christian creative minority in our own age faces a unique problem: How do we communicate the unique saving message of Christ to the world when the world attempts to shut us out of the normal means of social communications (television, newspapers, etc.)? And how do we shape culture if the traditional technologies used to communicate with our world are controlled by those who are unfriendly to Catholic teachings and ethical guidance?

I offer this simple solution: bypass the old media. New Media — the user-generated virtual world of Facebook, Twitter, and other social communications — creates the perfect, even playing field for Catholics to communicate the Good News. And when we face opposition, New Media enables us to break through that resistance by proclaiming the Gospel articulately, loudly, and in unison. Unlike traditional media, there are no gatekeepers on the Internet and social-media sites. There is only the ongoing search for meaning — the quest for that tiny mustard seed which develops into faith.

What follows is the blueprint I and others have put into action to equip Christians with modern technological tools to creatively communicate and defend the truth. My blog **American Papist** (www.AmericanPapist.com) is one of the most read Catholic blogs in the world. While I do discuss and comment on the Catholic news of the day, my specialty is uniting Catholics for the purpose of putting our faith into effective, coordinated action. I call this activity "Catholic online activism."

Three things are essential to conduct successful Catholic activism: faith, unity, and numbers. Why these three? Allow me to explain.

> *"Meanwhile, the power of the media to shape human relationships and influence political and social life, both for good and for ill, has enormously increased."[74]*
> — BLESSED JOHN PAUL II, MESSAGE FOR THE 37TH WORLD COMMUNICATIONS DAY (2003)
>
> *"The positive development of the media at the service of the common good is a responsibility of each and every one. Because of the close connections the media have with economics, politics and culture, there is required a management system capable of safeguarding the centrality and dignity of the person, the primacy of the family as the basic unit of society and the proper relationship among them."[75]*
> — BLESSED JOHN PAUL II, *THE RAPID DEVELOPMENT* (2005)

» 1. Faith

As the legal rule *"Nemo dat quod non habet"* declares, "No one gives what he does not have." If Catholics are to undertake online activism, they must work to build up their faith through frequenting the sacraments, reading Scripture, and studying the teachings of the Church. The better Christians we are, the better Catholic activists we will become. Catholic activism, because it involves communicating our faith to others, requires that we understand the truths we are attempting to articulate. Only when we have what we want to give — only when we have a strong faith — can we put that faith into action and build up the faith of others.

Prayer must constantly accompany and inspire our activism. Prayers know no distance; the Internet helps our prayers reach one another. Have you ever been sent an online request asking that you pray for an intention? Or have you ever begun an "online campaign" to solicit prayers for you or someone you know who needs them? Those are both small examples of Catholic spiritual activism: our faith in action online.

» 2. Unity

Jesus prays in the Gospel of John that his disciples "may all be one" (John 17:21). He has the same hope for his disciples today, yet sin and confusion continue to be obstacles for us. In order to be effective, the world needs to see the witness of our oneness. This means that we should exercise restraint when we disagree with other Catholics publicly, because we risk scandalizing the world when they see our disunity.

At the same time, we must also not shy away from addressing ignorance and falsehood. Making the right call in each situation takes patience and perseverance, but we must never forget Jesus' admonition that we should be "one."

Being "one" does not mean, of course, that all disagreements will disappear. It will remind us instead that as Catholics we do share the same faith and that at the end of the day we have more in common than not.

» 3. Numbers

After talking about faith and unity, "numbers" might strike you as a surprising third element for effective Catholic online activism. But they are extremely vital. By "numbers" I do not mean an "overwhelming majority." I mean enough individuals so that the force of what we are saying and doing compels notice by the wider culture. In our age, Christians are often silenced by being labeled as "extreme" and "fringe." We know, however, that a great number of good people believe as we do, and for good reason — because what we believe is true! The Internet and social media uniquely connect all of us united believers wherever we may be. This allows us to project a unified front to the world.

It is easy for the world to dismiss one person's argument or for the media to ignore a small group of activists. But I have found that it is impossible for the world to ignore a large, passionate, unified group of believers. We may be a minority, but that does not mean we are inconsequential and few. Instead it means each and every one of us needs to participate!

CatholicVote.org

Catholic social teaching holds that all Christians have a right and responsibility to participate in public life. The American bishops teach that such participation by all Christians, when able, is a moral obligation. Doing so allows us to shape the moral character of society, which is part of the mission given to us by Christ.

Today's political environment, unlike the past, is centered within the online world. Anyone running for office is assumed to have a Web presence, at a bare minimum, and more savvy candidates connect with voters through a variety of New Media tools.

With so much online political activity, it can be difficult to wade through partisan slogans and gimmicks. Since the Church's social teachings don't perfectly square with any political party, her voice can often be drowned out behind the noise of political advertisements and sound bites selected for their shock value.

In this political arena, where can Catholics turn to foster faithful citizenship? One website is the non-partisan **CatholicVote.org**, which fully follows the teaching and leadership of the Catholic Church. This lay-run group views political activity through the lens of Catholic social teaching, particularly by respecting the life and dignity of every human person and the sanctity of marriage. In a world with thousands of competing ideologies, this group stands as one of the few trying to offer a uniquely Catholic take on politics from a faithful, lay perspective.

The website's high-quality streaming videos — many of which have virally spread across the Catholic blogosphere — encourage a deeper consideration of Catholic social principles when voting. Their "Action Alerts" signal pressing pieces of legislation while linking you to your representatives so that your voice can be heard by decision makers. Their "Endorsement" page shows how different candidates stack up against the principles of Catholic social teaching, and their constantly updated blog covers current happenings in Catholic politics and culture.

In a political world where New Media is often used to promote ideologies counter to the Church's teaching, CatholicVote. org shows how these tools can instead encourage faithful activism.

Successful Internet Activism

Once Catholics unite together in strong faith and significant numbers, amazing things begin to happen. Here are some of the positive examples I've observed myself:

» Keeping the Witness of Mother Teresa Alive Today

In 2009, the U.S. Postal Service announced its intention to release a postage stamp commemorating the life of Blessed Teresa of Calcutta. Immediately, anti-religious groups began a campaign demanding that the USPS withdraw the stamp because they considered it an example of religious propaganda. In response, CatholicVote.org began an online countercampaign in support of the stamp. By the time it was released in September 2010, an online petition we created had compiled almost 150,000 signatures!

The large number of signers was due in part to the grassroots efforts of Catholics encouraging their friends to sign the petition online. Through the petition, the USPS realized that tens of thousands of Americans were eager to support and purchase the stamp, and on September 5, 2010, the stamp was released.

Catholics were able to help keep alive the witness of Mother Teresa's charity, and for each person, all it took was about 30 seconds and a desire to make a difference. This is a perfect example of the Catholic community in action, united around the amazing legacy of Mother Teresa, making her witness alive again today.

» **Organizing an Online Protest Against an Anti-Catholic Commercial**

Kayak, a popular website that searches for cheap airplane tickets, produced and aired an anti-Catholic TV commercial depicting two "repressed" nuns counting the days before they could escape their convent and break out their forbidden bikinis on a Caribbean party beach.

When I saw the ad, I blogged about it and explained why it was offensive. But then I took a second step — the activism step — explaining to my readers how they could use Facebook and Twitter to publicly tell Kayak that they were no longer going to use their services. Essentially, this was a street-side demonstration on Kayak's virtual property.

Virtual space, like physical space, matters. You show your commitment to a cause by physically going somewhere. Just think of the hundreds of thousands of pro-life Catholics who travel to attend the annual March for Life in Washington, DC.

They go somewhere — to our nation's capital — to show that unborn human life ought to be respected and protected. In a similar way, Catholics going to Kayak's Facebook page and Twitter feed showed that they believed Catholics should be respected in these online spaces, wherever people of goodwill are invited to gather.

As a result of our "online picket," Kayak pulled the offensive ad the very same day, and Kayak's chief marketing officer publically apologized. They had decided that as a business it was not worth alienating and offending their Catholic customers. Our efforts had more potential for success because we made it easy for Kayak to reconsider their actions — we "went" to them with our charitable, firm request.

» Singling Out Catholics for Mockery Isn't Fair Play

In June 2010, during the World Cup, I posted the video of an anti-Catholic ad produced by car manufacturer Hyundai that depicted a sacrilegious "soccer Mass." The offensive ad featured the worship of a soccer ball — a clear allusion to Eucharistic Adoration — and priests handing out pizza in lieu of the Eucharist during their "Mass."

Numerous Catholic blogs joined me, and together we formed an email campaign in response. Through our efforts in emailing Hyundai, they pulled the ad off the airwaves within 24 hours and sent notes of apology to everyone who contacted them. The anti-Catholic ad was ruled out-of-bounds because the collective online "stadium" of Catholic viewers made it clear that they felt they had been treated with disrespect and treated unfairly.

Our Catholic Faith in Action

Today's college atmospheres are charged with rival ideologies and partisan politics. Social debates — formal and informal —

are daily ritual on most campuses, while it's not uncommon to see shouting matches over social issues. Everyone has an opinion on how to structure the world in order to bring about a healthy and just society.

The Catholic Church's own body of social teachings rarely gets a fair shake in these environments. In fact, many within the Church consider her social wisdom to be her best-kept secret.[76] Many Catholics realize that the Church needs to spread her social teachings out to the world — especially into college settings — if they are to hold weight.

In order to help with this, the Catholic bishops of America have employed the tools of New Media. Their **Our Catholic Faith in Action** website (www.USCCB.org/Campus) is aimed, in particular, at college students and other young adults.

The website features videos of young leaders working for justice, podcasts on social-teaching themes, and links for deeper exploration. The site also offers downloadable prayers and small-group study programs to dig into the spirituality behind the Church's social philosophy.

To ensure authenticity, Our Catholic Faith in Action links to the foundational documents of Catholic social teaching — the many papal, synodal, and episcopal statements on justice issues. This allows anyone with an Internet connection to instantly engage the actual teachings themselves, rather than second-hand distortions.

Through Our Catholic Faith in Action, the Church is sharing her social teachings using the language of the modern world, ensuring that they no longer remain her "best-kept secret."

» Supporting Brave Bishops

Archbishop John Nienstedt of St. Paul and Minneapolis is a brave defender of the Church's teaching that marriage is the union of one man and one woman for life. When homosexual activists decided to demonstrate at a Mass he was celebrating, I asked Catholics to send Archbishop Nienstedt emails pledging prayers and support.

We sent almost 40,000 messages and were able to tell the archbishop that despite whatever criticism he was receiving — especially through unfriendly blogs and newspapers — he had the support of Catholics all across the country.

» Supporting Persecuted Christians

Asia Bibi is a Christian mother of five who was sentenced to death in Pakistan for "blasphemy" against Islam. When Pope Benedict called for her release, I asked my readers to join in emailing our U.S. government to come to Bibi's aid. We didn't single-handedly resolve the situation, but in this simple way we expressed solidarity with her cause and did something concrete on her behalf: praying for her deliverance. Our prayers and activism, when they take place through the Internet and social media, truly reach around the world.

» Advocating Pro-Life, Pro-Family Legislation

People in this country still talk about something called "the Catholic vote." It's the idea that Catholics take political action in a cohesive, faithful manner; that Catholics can be counted on, despite their diversity, to present a unified voting front. But this "Catholic vote" began falling apart in the 1960s and 1970s when Catholics gradually became indifferent toward Catholic social principles.

Today, however, this decline is slowly reversing. Active Catholics are more pro-life and pro-traditional marriage than their peers. And politicians have come to recognize how much support they can expect from these active Catholics if they work to defend the unborn and promote the family.

I have encouraged Catholics countless times to ask their elected representatives in Congress to support pro-life and pro-family legislation, and to vote for candidates that reflect Catholic values in their campaigns.

Since beginning this project, I've witnessed real, positive change. I've watched anti-life proposals defeated by close votes — where the margin of victory was likely decided by the efforts of the Catholic community. And I've had elected officials in government express to me their appreciation for the thousands of encouraging messages they've received from Catholics.

Becoming an Online Activist

These examples of what Catholic activism can accomplish represent only the tip of the iceberg. Think about any of the great injustices in the world today: Catholics have a real opportunity to help right these wrongs through their online activity, and it begins with the simplest of steps. Here are some easy ways you can immediately become an online activist:

1. **Visit websites that encourage Catholic online activism**, such as CatholicVote.org (where I blog), your diocesan website, or your state Catholic conference of bishops website. These pages often have action alerts related to legislation and elections in your state.

2. **Sign up for social-networking sites** such as Facebook and Twitter, and then pick good Catholic pages to "Like" and "Follow." (You can find me on Facebook at www.Facebook.com/AmericanPapist or on Twitter at www.Twitter.com/AmericanPapist). Social networks are an incredibly powerful way to share the Good News: you can share inspirational quotes from the saints, copy the Mass readings for the day, post important Catholic news stories, and help keep Catholics connected in other ways. Be careful not to overdo it: just remind yourself to bring your faith and identity with you when you go online.

3. **Sign petitions to support good causes** (such as the "Support the Mother Teresa Stamp" I mentioned above). It only takes a few moments, and it really does make a difference. A petition with a large number of signatures proves to those who are prone to doubt that many people really do care about an issue. After you sign a petition, encourage your friends to do the same. It is easy to copy and paste the petition link into your Facebook- or Twitter-status updates.

Catholic Relief Services

On January 12, 2010, a 7.0-magnitude earthquake rocked the impoverished land of Haiti. News about the tragedy spread around the world at light speed through Twitter, Facebook, YouTube, and blogs.

Immediately, people began contributing "micro-donations" online, charitable gifts at small increments. Almost every charity in Haiti set up online giving centers that allowed contributions to be made at the click of a button.

But one of the most impressive responses came through the use of text messages. By sending a text message to a charity's unique phone number, users could donate $5, $10, or other small amounts within seconds. In the first ten days, over $30 million was collected solely through text-message pledges.[77]

Catholic Relief Services (www.CRS.org), the international relief arm of the U.S. Catholic Church, has been using New Media in similar ways to educate and promote charitable giving.

"Social media is an exemplary platform where we can offer our supporters small actions they can take every day," says Laura Durington, CRS's online community manager. "We value the idea that the more informed our supporters are about the plight of the world's poor, the better for everyone."

CRS has a blog where they post stories and updates from their work around the globe, a Facebook page where people can converse about CRS's work, a Twitter account where they share quick news bites and web links of interest, and a YouTube channel.

These New Media tools proved especially important during the charity's relief work in Haiti.

"In the days and weeks that followed the earthquake, we saw our Facebook page jump from 6,000 members to nearly 15,000," Laura explains. "Facebook and Twitter became invaluable channels for us. While the media was reporting that no food was being distributed in Haiti, we were able to communicate that we were distributing food, water, tents, and tarps by posting pictures of these items being handed out. Because of the ease in which users can share and 're-tweet' our content, our supporters could easily share our posts with their networks, furthering our reach into the digital world."

4. **If you already write a blog, consider ways your writing could encourage people to take action, and write about issues that interest you.** If starting a blog seems too daunting, try commenting on other blogs you enjoy. This will help you to develop a thick skin, because people who comment on blogs do not always behave charitably. Still, it is worth the effort, and it is always a good thing to stand up for the truth, regardless of how it is received at the time.

5. **Write emails** (but don't "spam" your family members' and friends' inboxes with too many forwarded messages!). Email is still the basic way most of us communicate online. Many of the best stories I have written came to my attention through one of my readers sending me an

email alert. Also, many websites offer an email address where you can send online letters to the editor and short opinion pieces. This is a very effective way to get the truth out to an audience that might never encounter it otherwise. And many of the most successful campaigns I have encountered involved sending emails of either encouragement or criticism directly to the person or organization in question.

Online Catholic Activism — In Continuity With Our Faith and History

In his message for the 45th World Communications Day, Pope Benedict said about the Internet: "As with every other fruit of human ingenuity, the new communications technologies must be placed at the service of the integral good of the individual and of the whole of humanity."[78] If we wish to fully integrate our Catholic faith into our lives, we must also integrate our faith into our lives online, truly becoming faithful digital citizens.

I always like to conclude my explanation of online Catholic activism with a little analogy from the Bible. When the people following Jesus became too numerous, Jesus got on a boat — cutting-edge technology at the time — to better reach those crowds. He also used the boats provided by his first disciples to cross the sea, going wherever the people were who needed to hear him.

May our online activity become that little flotilla of boats that brings the saving message of Christ, even into the depths of the Internet.

Thomas Peters is the founder and writer of the **American Papist** blog, which is hosted at CatholicVote.org. He has appeared in dozens of TV, radio, and online media outlets. Since 2007, he has lived and worked in Washington, DC, and now serves as the cultural director at the National Organization for Marriage. He holds two graduate degrees in theology.

CHAPTER 11
// Moving Mountains: Building a Digital Movement //
Shawn Carney

In previous generations, social movements were slowly grown by word of mouth. Occasionally, some movements used newspaper accounts, expensive paid advertising, or public-service announcements. But in today's world, New Media tools allow the Church to rapidly rally large groups of Catholics to bring about a better society. In her promotion of the common good, the Church can use these powerful tools to build thriving movements of faith.

My wife, Marilisa, and I are privileged to be involved in engaging digital technology to generate such a movement. From humble beginnings in 2004, **40 Days for Life** (www.40DaysForLife.com) has utilized New Media to join hundreds of thousands of Catholics with believers across many other faith traditions in a worldwide movement to eradicate abortion. In this chapter, I will tell you how it happened and show the significant role New Media played.

The abortion industry in America is big — *really* big — with more than 1.5 million abortions a year. So ending abortion can seem hopeless, especially when you consider the money and power of the industry that profits from it. In their last reported year, Planned Parenthood, the nation's largest abortion provider, took in over $350 million dollars in tax funding alone. The abortion lobby is one of the most influential in Washington, DC, which means the overturning of *Roe v. Wade* — the court case that legalized abortion in 1973 — will take a very long time. Many in our nation, even Catholics, presume that abortion is here to stay. They think that it's a way of life, that it's just how things go.

> *"Finally, the promotion of dialogue through the exchange of learning, the expression of solidarity and the espousal of peace presents a great opportunity for the mass media which must be recognized and exercised. In this way they become influential and appreciated resources for building the civilization of love for which all peoples yearn."[79]*
>
> — POPE BENEDICT XVI, MESSAGE FOR THE 40TH WORLD COMMUNICATIONS DAY (2006)

> *"[I]t is gratifying to note the emergence of new digital networks that seek to promote human solidarity, peace and justice, human rights and respect for human life and the good of creation. These networks can facilitate forms of co-operation between people from different geographical and cultural contexts that enable them to deepen their common humanity and their sense of shared responsibility for the good of all."[80]*
>
> — POPE BENEDICT XVI, MESSAGE FOR THE 43RD WORLD COMMUNICATIONS DAY (2009)

Inspired Beginnings

While living in Bryan/College Station, Texas, I realized that prayer was the primary answer to the abortion crisis. During my senior year of college in 2004, my newly wedded wife and I had been asked by David Bereit to work for the Coalition for Life, a local pro-life organization. We had volunteered for the coalition all throughout college, and David was the organization's director. He and the small staff were frustrated at the increase of our local abortion numbers, so we gathered around a wooden table and spent one hour in prayer, asking for God's guidance on what to do.

Forty days — that's what came from that hour of prayer. It occurred to us how God had regularly used 40 days throughout history to call his people back to him — to chastise, to renew, to transform. This hour of prayer surfaced a burning question for

David, me, and Marilisa: *What if we dedicated 40 days to ending abortion in our community?*

So with a leap of faith, and only two weeks to plan before the college students returned for the fall semester, we decided to call our community to 40 days of prayer and fasting. We organized 40 days of community outreach by visiting churches and going door-to-door asking people to pray for an end to abortion, and we also sponsored a 40-day-and-night peaceful vigil outside our local Planned Parenthood abortion facility. Thus, in fall 2004, the first 40 Days for Life campaign was born in Bryan/College Station, Texas.

We thought this would exist as only one campaign in one community. But the power of the Holy Spirit and the power of digital media created a movement that none of us could have ever imagined. That first campaign gathered over 1,000 new people from our community. Secular media outlets gained new interest in the pro-life activities, and more importantly, our local abortion numbers dropped by 28 percent. God had truly begun to move mountains.

At the end of the 40 days, we were exhausted. Our volunteers were tired, and we never dreamed that people in another city might want to bring this effort to their community. After all, we did not feel equipped to manage them, train them, and teach them what worked and didn't work during our campaign. We knew that the problem of abortion was local, but it took the Holy Spirit to show us that the solution was local as well. We just had to find a way to make it available for people on a bigger scale.

Spreading the Word

After the fall 2004 campaign, David Bereit moved to Washington, DC, to work for a national pro-life organization, which left Marilisa and me in charge of the local organization in Bryan/College Station, Texas. Over the next three years, groups and individuals from across the country heard about our 40 Days for Life campaign and asked if we would help bring it to their communities. We gave them some direction and posted a simple informational packet on our website. As a result, six other communities conducted 40 Days for Life campaigns, mainly on their own.

Those campaigns saw similar results to those we had experienced in 2004. Lives were saved, media outlets were covering the campaigns, post-abortive women were finding healing, new volunteers were getting involved, and people who had served in the pro-life movement for years were filled with a renewed sense of hope.

I even spoke at a few of the 40 Days for Life campaign events in those other cities. I was excited to see others using our approach, our fliers, and even the original logo that David had designed in 2004. I was also humbled by the passion and determination of the leaders to use this campaign to help them do something about abortion in their communities.

It wasn't a mystery why they trusted the 40 Days for Life campaign: because it was based on prayer. After seeing six cities conduct successful 40 Days for Life campaigns, we began imagining the possibility of conducting nationally coordinated, simultaneous 40 Days for Life campaigns across America.

Fathers for Good

Many television programs depict fathers as selfish, pleasure-seeking fools — think Homer Simpson or Al Bundy. And besides depicting egotism as the norm, much of the media also encourage men to objectify women and to take lightly their roles as husbands and fathers. Sadly, these negative urgings have led many men to embrace and make real these warped caricatures of manliness.

The **Fathers for Good** digital movement (www. FathersForGood.org) — organized by the Knights of Columbus — aims at countering these distorted images of masculinity and fatherhood by helping men to become selfless, devoted dads and spouses. And the endeavor relies primarily on New Media to do so.

On the Fathers for Good website, visitors can interact in many ways: they can listen to a podcast discussing how to talk with teenage children about sex, ask parenting advice in the discussion forums, or read a blog article on balancing work and family.

"We seek an interactive relationship with our visitors, with a Facebook group, comment boxes in every posting, a father's blog, and an "ask the expert" question-and-answer forum," says Brian Caulfield, the website's editor. "We also use email 'blasts' to alert Fathers for Good members of new and interesting content."

Because of its seriousness and prevalence, pornography is one topic Fathers for Good particularly focuses on. A recent study revealed that 25 percent of all search-engine requests are pornography related,[81] while another showed that more than 70 percent of men ages 18-34 visit a pornographic site in a typical month.[82]

Caulfield explains that, "One of the most popular initiatives of Fathers for Good is a program called "Men are Stronger than Porn." There we talk bluntly about the destructive nature of apparently harmless porn, and have witnesses from men who have come back from the edge of addiction to tell their stories. We believe that with support and God's grace, men can win their personal battles, whether with porn or any other negative behavior."

Through online resources and dialogue, Fathers for Good is helping numerous men discover true masculinity and how to live as faithful husbands and fathers.

New Media Builds the Movement

With these bold goals, our attention turned to communication. In order to lead a 40 Days for Life campaign, people needed to be motivated and trained. They would also need regular communication with us, the other campaign leaders, and their local volunteers. This was going to require some good use of technology, especially since we were up against something as big, well funded, and tech-savvy as the abortion industry.

Thankfully, few in the pro-life movement knew how to use technology better than David Bereit. Before he began his work as a pro-life activist, he had built and used innovative websites, email lists, and telecommunication methods in the business world. David and I discussed how to reach as many people as possible to sign up for a 40 Days for Life campaign. We knew that technology and our ability to connect with people would determine whether this Spirit-led endeavor would be a success or fall dead in the water. Simply put, for this to work, we had to both put our faith in God and trust the technology he gifted us with.

In the beginning, we were just two guys with laptops and cell phones. But to launch a nationally coordinated campaign, we had to reach the masses. In spring 2007, we began hosting online webcasts where people could call in or listen on their computer. To be part of an online webcast, people were asked to register and give us their email address. This was key because email is the way we communicate, invite, and train people to participate in 40 Days for Life.

We could not make calls to Christians in every city asking them if they wanted to host a campaign in their local community. We had to connect with potential leaders across the country, identify the ones interested, and then inform them about how to be part of the national movement. But we couldn't do that solely through phone calls. Instead, we discovered that our webcasts were the best way to reach this huge group of potential leaders.

After hosting a few smaller pro-life webcasts, we held a big webcast called "Pro-Life Breakthrough." In it, we described 40 Days for Life, shared the results from the prior campaigns in the first six cities, and offered the opportunity to register for the first-ever nationally coordinated 40 Days for Life campaign in fall 2007.

We emailed invitations to the webcast attendees, explaining that applications to participate would be open for two weeks in late July. We had no idea what to expect. Quickly, however, the buzz began building on blogs, Christian media outlets, and the number of people who signed up skyrocketed.

But we wanted to stir excitement even more. We created an online Google map and put the city of everyone who had responded with interest on the map. When we emailed the map link to everyone on our contact list, the buzz increased even more. Individuals from 600 different cities expressed interest, even before the applications officially opened. More importantly, that map gave people hope that this movement could indeed spread across the nation.

For the national campaign, David and I had hoped to have 20 to 25 cities registered. We were amazed that, in the end, 89 cities in 33 states had officially applied to participate in the first-ever nationally coordinated 40 Days for Life.

Reel Love Challenge

According to a 2010 Pew Research poll, marriage is on the decline, especially among young adults.[83] The percentage of married 20-something's dropped from 68 percent in 1960 to just 26 percent in 2008. In addition, nearly 4 in 10 survey respondents claimed that marriage is obsolete. To make matters worse, if current trends continue, between 40 and

50 percent of people that marry today will eventually end up divorced.[84]

These sobering statistics have invigorated the **Ruth Institute** (http://www.RuthInstitute.org) — an organization promoting lifelong love — to reorient the views young people have toward marriage through the avenues of New Media.

"New Media is one of the most successful and potent ways to present our mission to students," says Jamie Gruber, executive director of the Ruth Institute. "We have found that students who hear our message through grassroot networks on various New Media markets are more likely to take our mission seriously. New Media has made our work more accessible to young people and more effective in changing the culture."

One of the Ruth Institute's most innovative projects is their **Reel Love Challenge** (www.RuthInstitute.org/ReelLoveChallenge), a film contest focused on the question "How is lifelong love possible?" The contest, which ran from September 2010 to February 2011, was open to any college student or young adult. Entrants filmed a 30-second video explaining marital love and then uploaded their videos to the Reel Love Challenge website. Online visitors then voted on their top 10 favorite videos, before a panel of judges selected the ultimate winners. Cash prizes worth $4,500 were given to the top three entrants, while five video cameras were also given away during the contest.

The Reel Love Challenge shows how New Media can display the beauty of self-giving love to a culture harboring low views of marriage and high views of technology.

"In a generation that wants to understand and live their faith," Jamie says, "New Media gives young people an outlet to influence their friends for Christ. These tools have opened a floodgate of opportunity for the Church that we must capitalize on."

Virtual Training and Communication

At the end of July, we immediately began training our local leaders on how to conduct the campaigns, reach out to churches, recruit volunteers, get permits, and communicate their efforts to the media. We had just six weeks to prepare 89 local city leaders, so we relied on the technology that had already served us well: webcasts and email. We held seven training webcasts on different topics, and within weeks our leaders were ready to kickoff 40 days of prayer, fasting, community outreach, and peaceful vigils outside abortion facilities.

Around this time, one of the most helpful New Media tools we began using was an online forum that was set up so our local leaders could communicate with one another. In the forum, we also posted press-release templates, fliers for church bulletins, and other resources to help them run their local campaigns. Each local leader was also given a 40 Days for Life website, based off of the national website so that all the local campaign websites had a consistent look and feel.

Anyone visiting the national website could quickly click on the campaign closest to them and were immediately put in contact with their local 40 Days for Life team. This created a huge network of advocates and gave leaders their own volunteer email list for their local community. Embracing the Catholic social-teaching principle of "subsidiarity," we used technology not to build a top-down empire but to empower the grassroots movement.

All of this technology helped the 89 locations to feel connected and united with other communities across the country. This was important to us because praying in front of an abortion facility alone, at 10:00 p.m., in the rain, can make anyone feel lonely. Prayer connected all of us, and technology displayed that unity to the rest of the world. God used this simple campaign built on basic principles right out of Scripture

— prayer, fasting, solidarity, and putting our faith into action — to build the largest pro-life movement in history.

Fulton Sheen's Cause for Canonization

Few Catholics in the 20th century had a greater or more visible impact on culture than Archbishop Fulton J. Sheen. Renowned as a theologian, philosopher, and writer, Archbishop Sheen was most known for his media work. From 1930 to 1950, Fulton Sheen's *Catholic Hour* radio show was beamed to more than four million people each week.[85] In 1951, he began his weekly television show, which attracted even more attention.

Soon after Archbishop Sheen's death, people were already clamoring to begin his cause for canonization, a long process usually taking many years. In order to become recognized as a saint — after the Church first declares a Catholic to be a "Servant of God" and then "Venerable" — a person must be beatified (making Archbishop Sheen, for example, "Blessed Fulton Sheen"). For this, a miracle attributed to the archbishop's intercessory prayers must be found. To be canonized — to be known as "St. Fulton Sheen" — requires another verified miracle.

To encourage more Christians to ask for Archbishop Sheen's prayers, a massive media effort began to push forward the movement. His cause for canonization stands as the first in Church history to truly harness New Media. And because Fulton Sheen dominated the media of his day, this use of technology seems most appropriate.

"The leadership behind Sheen's cause recognized that New Media is truly one of the primary modes of communication in this generation," explains Alexis Walkenstein, board member of the Archbishop Fulton Sheen Foundation. "Had Sheen lived today, he would likely have used New Media to evangelize."

Archbishop Sheen's campaign has been spearheaded by **The Maximus Group** (www.MaximusMg.com), a Catholic communications and marketing agency. They have used the full gamut of New Media tools to get their message out: a website (www.ArchbishopSheenCause.org), a blog (http://FultonSheen.blogspot.com), a Facebook page, and a Twitter account were created, each providing updates on his cause for canonization along with daily quotes from the holy man.

"Ultimately," Alexis says, "New Media, as used to promote a saint's cause, is a way to bring that man or woman of God to life in ways that were never before possible."

Expansive Growth

Following that fall 2007 40 Days for Life campaign, we immediately received requests from many cities hoping for a spring campaign during Lent. David and I had very little time to prepare and repeat what we had just done the previous fall. But we trusted that the same Spirit and technology which had worked in the fall would work in the spring.

During Lent 2008, we had 59 cities for the second coordinated 40 Days for Life campaign. From there, the movement continued to grow. The following fall we saw double the number of cities from the first fall, and the following spring we saw double the number from the first spring.

Since fall 2007, the results of 40 Days for Life as of publication are as follows:

- A total of 1,085 individual campaigns have taken place in 337 cities in all 50 states and 6 countries.

- More than 400,000 people have joined together in a historic display of unity to pray and fast for an end to abortion.

- More than 13,000 church congregations have participated in 40 Days for Life campaigns.

- Reports document 3,599 lives that have been spared from abortion — and those are just the ones we know about.

- Forty-three abortion workers have quit their jobs and walked away from the abortion industry.

- Nine abortion facilities have completely shut down following local 40 Days for Life campaigns.

- Hundreds of women and men have been spared the tragic effects of abortion, including a lifetime of regrets.

- More than 1,200 news stories have been featured in newspapers, magazines, radio shows, and TV programs from coast to coast and overseas.

- Many people with past abortion experiences have stepped forward to begin post-abortion healing and recovery.

After so many years of legalized abortion, many people of faith are experiencing a renewed sense of hope! David Bereit and I have visited over 300 of the 40 Days for Life locations, but we have not even begun to reach all those that God has touched through this technology-driven campaign.

40 Days for Life came about through an hour of prayer around an old wooden table in Texas. It arose from the Holy Spirit communicating to a few people what we were supposed to do to help end abortion in our community. Our intention was not to build a digital movement, but that was what the Spirit used to bring the movement to hundreds of thousands of people. Technology, when used properly and with a good conscience, can create roads that can lead to any important goal — even to the end of abortion in our world. If faithful Christians harness the power of New Media, even the biggest mountains can be moved.

Shawn Carney is the cofounder and campaign director of **40 Days for Life** (www.40DaysForLife.com). He is a regular media spokesperson and his work has been featured on hundreds of media outlets, including Fox News' *The O'Reilly Factor*, the *New York Times*, and the *Los Angeles Times*, and Christian media, including the *Christian Post*, the *National Catholic Register*, Salem Radio, Relevant Radio, EWTN Radio, and Focus on the Family.

Shawn also serves as executive producer and host of the new pro-life television series, *being HUMAN*, which airs in 128 million homes via the Eternal Word Television Network (EWTN).

Shawn and his wife, Marilisa, have four children.

// To Infinity and Beyond: The Future of the Church and New Media //
Brandon Vogt

Marshall McLuhan, a 1960s media prophet, was one of the first to observe the profound ways that technology shapes culture. Decades before the Internet became mainstream, McLuhan warned of the unintended effects brought by each new communication tool. His still-famous phrase "the medium is the message" summarizes his observations, pointing out that a particular medium shapes a message more than the content it carries.

For example, McLuhan, a late convert to Catholicism, would affirm that since each medium encourages different ways of thinking, a sermon delivered through radio, through television, through a blog, and through YouTube would be received in drastically different ways. The radio sermon would be listened to with sustained attention, the television sermon would be viewed as entertainment, the blog sermon would be shallowly skimmed, and the YouTube sermon would speak more emotionally and viscerally than the others.

Many Christians operate out of the belief that we can "communicate the same message through new means." They assume what McLuhan adamantly denied, that communication mediums can be neutral. For better or worse, however, New Media conditions whatever the Church shares through these technologies; how we think, relate, speak, read, worship, and pray are all influenced by these tools and the culture they create.

Throughout this book, we've seen numerous ways that New Media can strengthen the Church's missions of evangelization, formation, community, and the common good. Scores of

Catholic experts and innovators have showed how these tools are already being used well.

But what does the future hold for the Church and New Media? In what ways are these tools shaping both the future of the Church and the future of the world? We'll conclude by reviewing a handful of negative, future trends in the Church and New Media relationship — suggesting how the Church can respond to each — before balancing those with some positive future trends.

May we now gaze into the future, glimpsing how these New Media tools are affecting our faith.

Negative Future Trends (and How the Church Can Respond)

Both online and offline, you'll find no shortage of negativity, hostility, and hesitancy when it comes to engaging New Media. Many cultural observers have already warned of New Media's undesirable effects. For instance, critics note how over the last couple of decades, the Internet has extended one of the world's most ravaging vices: pornography. New Media's ease and quickness have amplified pornography's availability, damaging numerous men, women, and marriages along the way.

Also, pundits point to the vitriol and lies spread through the anonymity of New Media. In an article for the *New York Times*, a Facebook employee echoed this, chronicling the ways that online anonymity breeds contempt.[86] Many Internet users can attest that people seem much more likely to write angry messages online than speak them in person.

These New Media concerns are among the many that the Church will face in an increasingly digital future, but they aren't the only ones. What follows are five other significant trends, ways that New Media is negatively affecting the Church. Yet recognizing that these effects aren't unanswerable, each trend closes with suggestions on how the Church can respond:

» **Shallower Relationships**

In today's always-on, always-connected world, we have contact with more people than ever before. For instance, Twitter users have an initial 2,000 "follower" limit, while Facebook has a "friend" limit of 5,000 — and, yes, many people bump up against these constraints.

But despite these vast connections, many online relationships are shallow. New Media tends to cultivate relationships that are a mile wide and an inch deep, reducing relationships to sentence-long Facebook comments and 140-character tweets.

More troubling, this shallowness affects offline relationships as well. New Media's sporadic content makes it difficult to sustain long, in-depth conversations offline. Its encouragement to "click, go, skim, and tweet" makes it hard to simply "be." Whether sitting at the bedside of a sick friend, being present to a wife who just lost her husband, or listening to the musings of a young toddler, "being present" to others — without the need to fix, solve, respond, or check our phone — is difficult in our electronic culture.

Online relationships do provide at least one major upside, however. As children gradually welcome parents into their online world, they reveal problems, friendships, interests, and activities like never before. For many parents, the blogs, Facebook notes, and Twitter tweets have essentially pried the lock off their children's diaries.

But, recognizing shallower relationships both online and offline, how is the Church to respond? First, the Catholic Church, though a technological novice, is an "expert in humanity."[87] After all, she has thousands of years of experience with human relationships.

Harnessing her expertise, she must teach people anew how to have intentional offline connections. One way to cultivate these relationships is through the original Catholic social network: the parish. Communal gatherings like the Mass, small faith-sharing groups, and service-oriented ministries can all provide depth that is unavailable online.

Second, the Church can help revive the dying arts of letter writing, phone calls, and — though many young people will gasp — face-to-face conversation. Along with Blessed John Paul II, she should remind the world that "electronically mediated relationships can never take the place of direct human contact."[88]

Her voice should be one of the loudest, encouraging people to power down their cell phones and pick up a pen and some paper; for families to close their laptops and sit around the dinner table; and for individuals to stop blogging and instead join a small-group or service project.

Finally, in Jesus Christ, the Church has the living water, the well that springs up to eternal life (John 4:14). To a world panting for relational depth, the Church can offer the deepest relationship experienced on earth: that with the Divine.

» Information Overload

If you read everything there was to read on the Internet, 24 hours a day, 7 days a week, it would take you 57,000 years to finish.[89] If you wanted to bypass your e-reader and instead read all of that information in paperback form, your printed book would weigh more than 1.2 billion pounds and extend 10,000 feet, cover-to-cover.

As people become crushed beneath this digital avalanche, the Church must continue to echo Jesus' invitation: "Come to me, all who labor and are heavy laden," Jesus says, "and I will give you rest" (Matthew 11:28). Since the beginning, God has offered this rest through the "Sabbath," the one day during the week when there is no work, no struggle, no overload — only rest.

Just as Christians rest physically one day a week, resting digitally helps remedy information overload. When we turn off our cell phones, close our laptops, and unplug our electronic devices, we become free of the drive to consume, produce, and stay in the loop.

We also become aware that while New Media keeps us informed, filling our mind with endless facts, it doesn't necessarily produce wisdom or virtue. Ultimately, information overload — like an overload of food — will never satisfy. As Blessed John Paul II says, "Understanding and wisdom are the fruit of a contemplative eye upon the world, and do not come from a mere accumulation of facts, no matter how interesting."[90]

Parishes, youth groups, and young-adult ministries would do well to practice a group-wide "digital Sabbath," encouraging members to communally fast from electronics. Likewise, establishing a regular virtual fast at the diocesan level would be an emphatic promotion of temperance and silence.

» Rise in Narcissism and Pride

A man you went to high school with tells you that he just burnt his breakfast. A distant cousin shares her reaction to a recent awards show. A complete stranger invites you to take a survey about his personality.

One of the biggest complaints regarding New Media is that most of these tools are inherently narcissistic. Facebook — "What's on your mind?" — and Twitter — "What's happening?" — encourage users to share their every thought and action with the world. Dozens of tools tempt users toward introspection and pontification, yet barely any promote true other-centeredness.

In addition, these tools engender pride unlike any past technology. Digital "success" can be measured and compared against others online, and online merit can easily be gauged by the number of visits, downloads, "likes," followers, or view counts. Many associate these "numbers" with personal value or worth, making it easy to think highly of yourself when you have a large online platform.

In light of this online vanity, how does the Church bring about a Copernican revolution of the digital soul? To inject humility into New Media, the Church can promote two potent facets of Catholic spirituality: "serving the poor" and "dying to self."

The saints provide examples of these two strategies in action. Blessed Teresa of Calcutta staved off pride and narcissism through her radical care for the marginalized. By serving others, she demonstrated how we can turn our inward focus outward, how we can turn away from our own agendas, thoughts, and desires toward those of others.

When it comes to "dying to self," St. Thérèse of Lisieux and her "Little Way" show us that success comes not through big things — not through thousands of blog readers or hundreds of downloads — but through small actions done with deep love. Thérèse and the Church can remind Christians that it's not about the numbers but about how faithful you are in using New Media.

Finally, and most powerfully, the Church can emphasize the humility of the Blessed Mother, who more than anyone else understood that her life wasn't about her. Pointing to Mary's words during the wedding feast at Cana, the Church can encourage New Media users to follow Jesus' direction, not their own (John 2:5). "Do whatever he tells you" is good advice for all Catholic New Media users today.

» Online Relativism

Most college professors and high-school teachers shun Wikipedia — a communal online encyclopedia — rejecting it as a legitimate source for facts. Most online users, however, have little problem trusting the site. A recent Pew Internet poll revealed that 53 percent of adult Internet users refer to Wikipedia when looking up information.[91]

A main reason for Wikipedia's contentious reputation is its communal nature: anybody, anywhere can edit just about any topical entry on the site. This democratic nature of Wikipedia shows a profound shift in the way our culture understands truth.

In past ages, objective truth — truth that never changes and applies to everyone, everywhere — found its basis in God and the Church. In our postmodern, Wikipedia world, however, objective truth has mostly fallen out of favor. Now, more than ever, truth and morality are simply defined by the majority opinion. If most people agree on the Wikipedia definition for a given topic, then it must be true. Likewise, many New Media users think, "If most of my Facebook friends, Twitter cohorts, and fellow bloggers support same-sex marriage, torture, and contraception, then those behaviors can't *really* be immoral."

The "digital continent" is dangerously vulnerable to this type of relativism. In New Media spheres, whoever is loudest becomes the authority — your credentials are the number of readers, followers, or listeners that you have.

But the Church has long counseled that while democracy is a valid form of government, it cannot be used when it comes to truth and morals. Reminding New Media users of objective truth, she must help her flock to discern fact from fiction online. And she must teach them how to measure online claims against Christian tradition. Instituting some type of online *Imprimatur* — a mark ensuring that content is free of doctrinal or moral error — may help.

Despite this online relativism, the Church must still pull up a chair to the online table and thrust her voice into the conversation. As Father Barron explained in Chapter 1, the Catholic tradition is intelligent, beautiful, and rich. She should be confident that her truths, through reason and experience, will prevail on the "virtual Areopagus."

» Difficulty in Prayer and Contemplation

New Media compels us, in the spirit of Jesus' friend Martha, to juggle "many things" (Luke 10:41). Upon opening our Internet browser, we're quickly swept into a torrent of links, articles, videos, downloads, pictures, and emails. A link within an article bounces us to another site, and the end of one YouTube video suggests another, so we explore the Web without centering our attention for more than a couple of minutes.

In his book *The Shallows*, author Nicholas Carr explains how our digital culture has literally rewired our brains to make us even better at these tasks.[92] The more we multitask and skim, the better we get at those same tasks.

Unfortunately, though, this rewiring shifts brainpower away from other mental spheres. We become incapable of performing tasks we don't regularly practice. Therefore, electronic culture has atrophied our capacity for critical thought, in-depth argument, reason, and logic.

New Media's scattered, unfocused nature clashes most with Christianity's rich practice of prayer and contemplation. In a world where most people take a pass on YouTube videos longer than five minutes or blog posts longer than a few paragraphs, how can the Church encourage people to center themselves in prayer?

As people become more absorbed in digital activity, the Church can urge practices like *lectio divina*, contemplative prayer, and Eucharistic Adoration to answer the Internet's distractions. While these devotions seem inefficient, unproductive, and pointless through the lens of electronic culture, they form the basis of a peaceful life.

Ultimately, the Church needs to remind New Media users that it was Mary, not Martha, who was right: there is need of only *one* thing. And that thing is union with Christ, whom we meet in undistracted silence.

Positive Future Trends (and What They Mean for the Church)

Despite these future negative effects, New Media holds tremendous potential for good. Many Church leaders have started to recognize this opportunity. Pope Benedict XVI, in particular, has centered many of his recent World Communications Day messages on these powerful tools. And in late 2010, he established the Pontifical Council for Promoting the New Evangelization.

Similarly, the pope has announced that the theme for the 2012 Synod of Bishops will be "New Evangelization." The synod will undoubtedly discuss ways that New Media can be used to carry forth the mission of the Church.

We'll now explore some of the many positive ways that New Media is affecting the Church, now and in the future:

» "Springtime" of Evangelization

No great evangelists of the past two millennia could have conceived that within minutes they could have their messages beamed to billions of people across the world, cheaply and instantly. St. Paul, the early Church Fathers, St. Francis Xavier, and Archbishop Fulton Sheen each would have given their right arm for access to our New Media.[93]

These technologies have birthed a "springtime" of evangelization in the world. People who would never consider setting foot in a church are dialoguing with priests on YouTube (see Chapter 1). Streaming videos and interactive websites encouraging inactive Catholics to return to the Church have already produced staggering results (see the "Catholics Come Home" sidebar in Chapter 1). And New Media is connecting the Church with many other difficult-to-reach groups: youth, young adults, the elderly and homebound, and those living in remote locations.

Young people, in particular, are often considered the most difficult demographic for the Church to evangelize. Yet, over 96 percent of young adults have joined a social network,[94] providing the perfect arena for the Church to meet them. Outside of New Media, there has hardly been a more powerful evangelistic tool to reach young people.

Also, though the virtual anonymity of New Media can be seen as a detriment, it can also be considered beneficial. Back in the 20th century, radio and television allowed Archbishop Fulton Sheen to reach a myriad of people who would never darken the doors of a church. Through Archbishop Sheen's programs, however, they could engage Catholicism in the privacy of their own homes, avoiding public embarrassment or critique.

New Media provides this same dynamic of evangelizing through anonymity. People uneasy about religion feel comfortable exploring Christianity behind the safety of their computer screens.

The Church does advise, however, that true witness is always personal; that online evangelism should optimally lead to personal dialogue and relationship. Properly termed, then, this New Media outreach is more "pre-evangelization" than "evangelization," but it does provide a monumental first step through doors — and screens — that have long been closed to religion.

» Innovative Faith Formation

"Just Google it." If you've been online for any amount of time, you've likely heard those words. On the Internet, you can easily find information about anything under the sun. This ever-growing repository of information has huge implications for faith formation.

First, New Media has removed the geographic and time constraints placed on traditional faith formation. In the old environment, Catholics looking to learn more about their faith had to travel to a specific place — a parish-life center or a lecture hall, for example — at a specific time. Now, through the power of the Internet, neither of those constraints exist.

The Church is just beginning to grasp the significance of this shift. John Roberto, author of the book *Faith Formation 2020*, explains, "We haven't yet wrapped our heads around the idea that we can reach people 24/7, anytime, anywhere."

The possibilities are almost endless. Asian Catholics can stream the pope's weekly address on their cell phones, while Catholics in Canada can download daily reflections from a priest in Nigeria. Catechists and teachers can carry the Bible, the *Catechism*, commentaries from the Church Fathers, past papal encyclicals, and a library of modern texts all on a device that fits in their pocket. And Catholic blogs and podcasts offer streams of quality religious content.

Besides just making all of this rich material available, however, New Media has turned the tables on how it is delivered. Before the New Media revolution, people sought information in books, pamphlets, and static websites. Now the information comes to them. RSS readers bring blog posts to one central location, YouTube videos go viral across the web, and social networks set the tone and topic for religious discussion.

In the digital revolution, the Church's challenge is not to get more people to come to classes on parish grounds but to fill the New Media stream with authentically Catholic content. By strategically moving into social networks, the Church's beauty, goodness, and truth will pop up in Facebook feeds, Twitter streams, and YouTube playlists across the world.

It has never been easier, quicker, or cheaper to explain the truths of Christianity than it is today, a realization that should excite all those charged with teaching the faith.

» Rise in Church Dialogue

Imagine a bishop responding to Tweets posted by people in his diocese, or a priest using Facebook to discuss his Sunday homily. This type of online interaction between clergy and laypeople isn't too much of a stretch. In fact, it is already happening in many places. New Media is already breathing fresh life into communications between Church leaders and laypeople.

One major theme throughout the Church's teachings on media is the value of dialogue. In recent centuries, numerous Church leaders have explained that the Church must be in constant conversation with the world, including both Catholics and non-Catholics. And this conversation, by its very nature, can't be one-sided; it must be an authentic, two-way dialogue.

Traditionally, Church leaders have communicated through homilies, personal letters, and episcopal statements. Today, however, the digital world expects to respond and engage with those speaking with them. Instead of passively receiving information, online Catholics want to discuss it.

Admittedly, dialogue brings with it a couple of dangers. The first is that it potentially flattens structures of authority. As mentioned in the "negative trends" section, it tends to promote an egalitarian state where the authority of ordained leaders is not always honored. For instance, if bishops — the ordained shepherds of the Church — dialogue through New Media, they run the risk of their voice becoming just "one of many."

Second, online religious dialogue almost always evokes detractors. As Father Robert Barron attests through his many interactions on YouTube, the large majority of commenters and questioners are anti-authority, anti-religious, or anti-Catholic (or all three). Instead of worrying whether detractors will arise, however, leaders should assume they will, and then prudently decide how to best engage them. What they shouldn't do is let the fear of detraction prevent any type of discussion.

If dialogue is practiced in full awareness of these dangers, it can flourish. Dialogue is at the heart of growth and community, both secularly — see Socrates — and religiously — see Jesus. Discussion gives the Church a human element, revealing her to be a living organism rather than a static institution.

Through prudent New Media dialogue, leaders can help people develop a closer relationship to the Church, and therefore to Christ. New Media users will experience what two travelers experienced almost 2,000 years ago: "While they were talking and discussing together, Jesus himself drew near and went with them" (Luke 24:15).

» Fresh Wave of Religious Vocations

Today, when someone researches a particular company, the first place they usually turn is to the Internet. Likewise, when a Catholic is trying to find a local parish, many look online, gauging a parish simply by its website.

So it should come as no surprise that for many people discerning religious vocations, the Internet plays a big role in their discernment process. A recent survey revealed that 90 percent of those discerning a religious vocation said their inquiries were aided by the Internet.[95] That same survey showed that a religious community's website was more essential than vocation directors, parish priests, parents, or friends when gathering vocational information. Simply put, the first place many people turn in their discernment process is not to a spiritual director but to Google.

Why is this? One reason is New Media's anonymity, as mentioned before. It allows users to comfortably explore things they would normally be hesitant to approach. A young woman might be uneasy about visiting a convent or committing to a discernment retreat, but in the comfort of her home she feels free to explore the characteristics of different religious orders.

Vocation Match (www.VocationMatch.com) is one example of this in action. The site asks visitors a set of questions regarding personality type, living conditions, prayer styles, and hobbies, and then uses the answers to suggest compatible religious organizations. The site shows how technology can help discern God's call. Other sites, like **For Your Vocation** (www. ForYourVocation.org), similarly use New Media to aid those discerning their vocation.

Dioceses wondering how to use New Media in this regard can imitate the successes of the Diocese of Bridgeport, Connecticut. Since the diocese began a vocational outreach page on Facebook, its number of seminarians has doubled.[96]

Finally, religious orders that have embraced New Media can expect a rise in interest. For example, the Daughters of St. Paul, the Paulist Fathers, and the Society of the Holy Child Jesus are all examples of religious orders with a strong New Media presence.

Vocations won't increase solely because a diocese or religious order has an attractive website or is active on Facebook. But just as New Media serves to pre-evangelize — a first step in the process of evangelization — so can New Media act as a vocational catalyst.

» Revolutionizing the Common Good

In early 2011, protesters in Egypt harnessed New Media to power their democratic revolution. Bloggers raised support for labor strikes, Facebook users coordinated massive marches, and Twitter tweets streamed up-to-the-second news. Citizens of Tunisia similarly used New Media to instigate profound social change.

These examples highlight New Media's power to facilitate large-scale movements, gatherings, and missions. In today's world, a college-student with a Facebook account has more networking power than Caesar Augustus, Genghis Kahn, or Alexander the Great. He can gather more people, more quickly, with less cost than any of those great leaders.

Likewise, in less than seven years, Facebook founder Mark Zuckerberg has connected one-thirteenth of humanity into a single network.[97] And a Facebook application called "Causes" helps charitable groups to acquire exposure and donations through these vast connections.[98] With so many people linked online — poor and rich, young and old, farmers and bankers and more — New Media's potential for compassion is vast.

Microlending provides just one example. In this system, low-interest loans — usually $50-$500 — are offered to entrepreneurs in developing countries. This small amount of seed money is often enough to help poor people lift themselves out of poverty. After the business takes off, the entrepreneur pays back the loan, allowing the funds to be re-loaned to someone else.

Microlending has proved very successful with its founder, Muhammad Yunus, winning the 2006 Nobel Peace Prize for popularizing the system. In recent years, New Media has opened up microlending to the world, allowing anyone, anywhere to participate. Internet sites like **Kiva.org** allow an American suburbanite to loan money to a baker in Ecuador or a cattle breeder in Kyrgyzstan. Through just a couple mouse clicks, a teenager can provide seed money for a retail store in Peru or a beekeeper in Uganda.

Other examples of New Media compassion include online campaigns, which use crowd-sourced donations toward a specific cause, and sites like **TheCommon.org**, a social network connecting local needs and abilities. In addition, the 2010 Haitian earthquake showed how New Media can effectively respond to unforeseen disasters (see the Catholic Relief Services sidebar in Chapter 11).

In the coming years, New Media will mobilize people around common causes as never before. For the Church, this means her rich traditions of charity and justice will be both empowered and digitized. Compassion will still require a person-to-person exchange, but the exchanges will be increasingly facilitated through New Media.

Conclusion

More than 500 years ago, Johannes Gutenberg — a Catholic — used New Media to change the world of his day. With our New Media, the same potential exists for us. Understanding this produces both excitement and a summons: because of New Media's ubiquity, the Church cannot afford to sit out this digital revolution.

She must enter the digital dance with prudence, courage, and invigoration. She must gather her nets and cast them wide into New Media's deep waters. She must shout loudly from the rooftops of the virtual world. And to New Media users, she must echo the roars of Blessed John Paul II: "Do not be afraid!"

Even as we're intimidated by New Media's novelty, fearful of its dangers, and complacent toward its change, we *must* use these tools. Few other means connect the Church with unreached populations, communicate the Gospel so innovatively and effectively, link communities across the world, and organize movements for good.

Now that you've encountered New Media's power and potential, may you join the Church in this great mission, an adventure for the ages. Using blogs, Facebook, Twitter, YouTube, podcasts, and the many other tools, may you release the explosive, captivating, liberating message of the Divine Medium: Jesus, our Lord.

> *"I extend the invitation which ... I have wished to express to the entire world: 'Do not be afraid! Do not be afraid of new technologies!' "*[99]
>
> — BLESSED JOHN PAUL II, *THE RAPID DEVELOPMENT* (2005)

Brandon Vogt is a Catholic writer and speaker who blogs at **The Thin Veil** (www.ThinVeil.net). His blog focuses on spirituality, technology, and social justice, and it features regular book reviews and weekly giveaways. He also manages the **Church and New Media** blog (www.ChurchAndNewMedia.com) and daylights as a mechanical engineer. Brandon and his wonderful wife, Kathleen, live in Casselberry, Florida, with their two children, Isaiah and Teresa.

Afterword
Archbishop Timothy M. Dolan

Did you know that decades before the dawn of the Internet, blogs, YouTube, and social networking (what we now call New Media), the Catholic Church was calling for their *invention*?

The *Compendium of the Social Doctrine of the Church*, summing up for us more than 75 years of the Church's consistent teaching regarding the mass media, states that one of the great moral principles society should aspire to is that of giving a voice to as many people as possible:

> Among the obstacles that hinder the full exercise of the right to objectivity in information, special attention must be given to the phenomenon of the news media being controlled by just a few people or groups. This has dangerous effects for the entire democratic system when this phenomenon is accompanied by ever-closer ties between governmental activity and the financial and information establishments.[100]

Here in America we all remember the day, not long ago, when an elite group of news anchors was the principal conduit of information for the entire nation. They delivered to us, in 30-minute evening broadcasts, what they considered we should know about what happened in the world that day. Those days of hyper-filtration of information by a select few are over, and according to the tradition of the Church, that is good news.

In this light, it was curious to witness much of the secular media respond with shock and awe when our beloved Holy Father, Pope Benedict XVI, recently released his message for the 45th World Communications Day of June 5, 2011, in which he invited Christians "confidently and with an informed and responsible creativity, to join the network of relationships which the digital era has made possible."[101]

Such expressions of surprise emanate from a false assumption that the pope is somehow breaking from the Church's traditional views and embracing for the first time the perilous, secular world of mass media. But, in fact, the Holy Father's words are wholly in sync with each of his predecessors' contributions to the issue, dating back to 1929, when the Church's Magisterium made its first solemn pronouncement about the mass media.[102] Since then, the Vatican has issued no less than 156 official statements regarding media production and consumption. These include systematic theological and ethical analyses by two encyclical letters, one conciliar decree, two pastoral instructions, and 45 papal messages for World Communications Day.[103]

Without exception, in these contributions the Church invites us to celebrate, not avoid, the possibilities new technology offers us for preaching the Gospel and promoting genuine human development.

The invitation to take advantage of these new opportunities is meant for all of us. In 1971, the Pontifical Commission of Social Communications called for pro-active engagement with the media at every level of the Church:

> As representatives of the Church, bishops, priests, religious, and laity are increasingly asked to write in the press or appear on radio and television or to collaborate in filming. They are warmly urged to undertake this work, which has consequences that are far more important than is usually imagined. But the complexity of the media requires a sound knowledge of their work, of their impact and of the best way to use them. It is therefore the task of the national centers and of the specialized organizations to make certain that those who have to use the media receive sufficient and timely training.[104]

I would be remiss if I didn't also note here the Church's resolute reminders of the accompanying moral obligations these new opportunities impose upon us. The Church points to the responsibility of mass media to educate and even entertain in a way that seeks the truth, respects the dignity of the human person, teaches virtue over vice, and promotes the common good of society.

But as Brandon Vogt and the contributors to this excellent book eloquently reveal, the Church's major challenge today is not that of educating her members about the real dangers of new technology — these are now self-evident — but rather of choosing to use it for the good, and learning to use it well. My hope and expectation is that this book will give the Church courage and wisdom to embrace New Media as one of the premier gifts of God to evangelists of our day.

And as Christians, we are all evangelists, implored by our friendship with God and his love for humanity to invest this gift wisely. My friends and family know I am not a "techie" by any stretch of the imagination. In fact, I still haven't figured out my television's remote control, and I fear someone will want to upgrade it before I ever figure this one out! Yes, our brave new world of technology and communication can be overwhelming in its complexity and consequences. And here lies the temptation for the contemporary Church: faced with a technological evolution beyond our personal capacities or preferences, we can opt for old and comfortable patterns of communication even if they limit our ability to connect in meaningful and effective ways with the world we are called to evangelize.

I call this a temptation because preferring comfort to mission is never a holy option. We need only imagine how the great evangelist, St. Paul, would utilize New Media as a tool to spread the Good News!

Adapting our communication of the Gospel to the world's needs is a demand that flows from our baptism in Christ and, believe it or not, in reference to bishops, it is even a law of the Church. In Canon 822, the revised Code of Canon Law summarizes the local bishop's obligation to use the media for the good:

> §1 In exercising their office, the pastors of the Church, availing themselves of a right which belongs to the Church, are to make an ample use of the means of social communication.[105]

The Second Vatican Council also charges bishops, as successors to the apostles, to use mass means of communication in the fulfillment of their task as the primary teachers of the faith in their dioceses. I am struck by the forceful language the council uses; it is yet another unsubtle cue to us that our involvement in mass media is not optional:

> [...] to announce the Christian doctrine, let them [the bishops] have recourse to public declarations [...] made through the press and the various instruments of social communication, which absolutely must be made use of for announcing the Gospel of Christ.[106]

As the archbishop of New York, there is no way I can fulfill this sacred obligation of effective evangelization alone. I depend on the many talented and enthusiastic priests, religious, and lay men and women who are ahead of the curve in using New Media for the sake of the Gospel. I know this is the experience of many of my brother bishops as well — we need you. We need you to go out ahead of us and to bring us with you!

Most Reverend Timothy M. Dolan

Archbishop of New York

Glossary

Many of these terms are notoriously hard to define, especially in down-to-earth language. The best effort was made to provide the simplest, most common definition of each term.

- ***Blog*** — Short for "web log," an interactive website with regular articles in reverse chronological order. Individual articles are called "blog posts," "posts," or "entries." Most blogs allow feedback from readers through comment boxes.

- ***Comment Boxes (comboxes)*** — The location on websites or blogs where readers can offer their responses to a particular piece of content or dialogue with other commenters.

- ***Domain Name*** — The online location of a particular website (i.e., what you type into an Internet browser to get to a particular site). For example, "www.osv.com" and "www.churchandnewmedia.com" are domain names.

- ***Download*** — To transfer a file or program from the Internet to your computer or other electronic device.

- ***Facebook*** — The most popular social network; a place where users can connect and communicate with friends by sharing comments, messages, photos, links, and video.

  » ***Facebook Page/Group*** — Special Facebook accounts used to promote businesses, parish activities, blogs, bands, or anything else seeking to build an audience.

  » ***Facebook Profile*** — The most common type of Facebook account, typically used by individuals instead of groups.

  » ***Facebook Wall*** — The place on each Facebook profile or page where Facebook users can share content. The content shared on a Facebook wall is usually a message, link, picture, or video.

Facebook walls can be public or private, depending on the user's privacy settings.

- ***Forum/Message Board*** — An online discussion site where messages, questions, and topics may be posted and replied to.

- ***Hosting (web, podcast, etc.)*** — Digital storage space where the data and files displayed by websites, blogs, and podcasts are stored. When creating a website or a podcast, you typically need both a domain name and a hosting service.

- ***Link*** — Transports Internet users from one website to another.

- ***Micro-blog*** — A blog featuring short, rapid posts (e.g., Twitter).

- ***New Media*** — New forms of on-demand, Internet-based communication that promote connectivity and interactivity.

- ***Podcast*** — Stemming from "iPod" and "broadcast," a series of digital media files — audio or video — accessed over the Internet. Audio podcasts can be thought of as radio-on-demand, since podcast episodes can be listened to anywhere, anytime and can be played, paused, rewound, or fast-forwarded at leisure.

- ***RSS Feed*** — A special feature on blogs, websites, online newspapers, or podcasts that delivers new content to an RSS Reader instead of forcing users to visit each individual site to check for new updates.

- ***RSS Reader*** — An aggregator that collects RSS feeds into one central location (e.g., Google Reader).

- ***Social Media*** — A specific subset of New Media that promotes dialogue, sharing, and online community.

- **Social Network** — A system that connects a group around common interests or needs (e.g., Facebook, MySpace, and LinkedIn).

- **Twitter** — The Internet's most popular micro-blogging application which requires each posted message to be 140 characters or less.

  » **Tweet** — A single message posted by a Twitter user.

  » **Hashtag** — A specific category that Twitter users can assign to a tweet (e.g., #cathmedia). Twitter users can search for specific hashtags to find tweets regarding a particular topic.

- **Upload** — To transfer a file or program from your computer or other electronic device to the Internet.

- **Vidcast (Videocast)** — A specific type of podcast that features video episodes instead of audio.

- **Web 2.0** — A general term describing the modern wave of online applications which feature interactivity and a two-way flow of information.

- **Website** — A collection of pages or documents on the Internet that form a single system.

- **YouTube** — The Internet's most popular video-sharing website. Any user can upload videos to the site, allowing others to watch them anywhere, at anytime, for free.

Appendix

Book Recommendations

Andriacco, Dan. *Screen Saved: Peril and Promise of Media in Ministry*. Cincinnati: St. Anthony Messenger, 2001. Print.

Carr, Nicholas G. *The Shallows: What the Internet Is Doing to Our Brains*. New York: W.W. Norton, 2010. Print.

Challies, Tim. *The Next Story: Life and Faith after the Digital Explosion*. Grand Rapids, MI: Zondervan, 2011. Print.

Gan, Eugene. *Infinite Bandwidth: Encountering Christ in the Media*. Steubenville, OH: Emmaus Road Publishing, 2010. Print

Hipps, Shane. *Flickering Pixels: How Technology Shapes Your Faith*. Grand Rapids, MI: Zondervan, 2009. Print.

———. *The Hidden Power of Electronic Culture: How Media Shapes Faith, the Gospel, and Church*. El Cajon, CA: Youth Specialties, 2006. Print.

Postman, Neil. *Amusing Ourselves to Death: Public Discourse in the Age of Show Business*. New York: Penguin, 2005. Print.

Roberto, John. *Faith Formation 2020: Designing the Future of Faith Formation*. Naugatuck, CT: LifelongFaith Associates, 2010. Print.

Swaim, Matt. *Prayer in the Digital Age*. Liguori, MO: Liguori Publications, 2011. Print.

Catholic Parish Website Designers

www.CatholicWebsiteDesign.com
www.eCatholicChurches.com
www.OSVoffertory.com/Radius.aspx
www.ParishGeeks.com
www.ParishWebAssistant.com
www.SolutioSoftware.com

Catholic New Media Conferences

Catholic New Media Celebration (http://CNMC.sqpn.com)
CatholiCon (www.CatholiConExpo.com)
Interactive Connections (http://mysite.verizon.net/res7geoo)

More Catholic New Media Resources

Catholic Media Guild Blog (www.CatholicMediaGuild.com) — New Media tips and articles for Catholics.

Catholic New Media Library (http://www.NCRegister.com/blog/
  Catholic_New_Media_Library) — Digital library of Church
  teachings related to New Media.
Catholic Tech Talk (www.CatholicTechTalk.com) — An online
  community for Catholics interested in technology.
Mobile Catholics (www.MobileCatholics.com) — Catholic resources for
  smart phones and other mobile devices.
Open Source Catholic (www.OpenSourceCatholic.com) — The go-to
  site for Catholic techies and web developers.
Teach Parents Tech (www.TeachParentsTech.org) — A Google-run
  site that uses short videos to answer many typical tech-related
  questions.

Acknowledgments

This project was purposely a symphony, not a solo — I may have conducted, but many others helped play the music. Thanks to each of the New Media innovators who shared their insights within this book. I'm especially grateful to Angela Santana, Matt Warner, Father Robert Barron, and the Word on Fire team, each of whom inspired the book significantly.

Also, thanks to the thousands upon thousands of faithful online Catholics who are blogging, podcasting, videocasting, networking, and tweeting the Kingdom of God to earth. Though I don't have space to thank you each by name, know that the gates of hell are crumbling against the force of our digital faith — may we "cast wide our nets" and "be not afraid"!

Specifically, the following people deserve my deepest gratitude:

Bert Ghezzi: You lit the fuse, then doused it in gasoline — I owe you my fire. Your brotherhood has refined me in every way. Thank you, my dearest friend.

Our Sunday Visitor: Thanks for trusting a young, first-time author to produce this book. I'm so grateful for your confidence.

Panera Bread in Altamonte Springs: Your wireless Internet, Diet Pepsi, and chocolate chip cookies fueled this effort. Thanks for providing a welcome home-base.

FSU Wesley Foundation: You introduced me to the Christ behind this book. Thanks for unveiling my eyes.

Vance Rains: You've influenced my Christian life more than anyone else, providing spiritual formation, virtuous example, and perennial encouragement. I'm honored to be your friend.

Brother Jason Zink: If I wasn't Catholic, this book wouldn't exist. I can never thank you enough for guiding me into the Church. St. Lawrence, pray for us both!

Dr. Tom Neal: You've shown me how to submit my intellect, will, and imagination to the Lord — to love as a husband, sacrifice as a father, and dream like a scholar. Thanks for being a hero.

St. Mary Magdalen Catholic Church (Altamonte Springs, Florida): If it wasn't for you, I wouldn't have the Eucharist each day. Thanks for feeding my soul and uniting me with Christ.

Monsignor Ed Thompson: You've never used a computer, never held an iPod, and have trouble with your cell phone. But you love Jesus Christ more than anyone I know, which is precisely why I love you. Thanks for your spiritual direction, your deep friendship, and for the many stacks of books.

Father Charlie Mitchell: Every time I've talked with you, I've left feeling like a saint. Thanks for the endless encouragement and support.

Father Rick Voor: You were the first priest I ever met who recited the Liturgy of the Hours, in Latin, using an iPhone. Answering the pope's call, you showed me a priest for the digital age.

Blessed John Paul II: It's because of you that I'm not afraid. Your courage and prophecy still reverberate in the online world. Thank you for your witness to hope.

Pope Benedict XVI: For guiding the Church across the "digital continent" and giving the Internet a soul, thank you. You've taught me how to display the face of Christ through every medium, in every age.

St. Francis de Sales, St. Isidore of Seville, and Servant of God Fulton Sheen: This book grew through your prayers and your communion. Thanks for lifting me onto your shoulders.

My Family: I love each of you dearly. For your relentless support — and timely babysitting! — I'll never adequately thank you. Thanks for raising and forming me into the man that I am.

Isaiah and Teresa: I'm sure you'll look back on this book and laugh while fiddling with your high-tech gizmos in the year 2030. Please don't think Daddy was a *complete* nerd (just partly).

Kathleen: You drive me, inspire me, invigorate me, and delight me more than any digital tool ever could. I'm so thankful for your sacrifice and encouragement each day during the book process, especially the difficult ones. I love you beyond measure, my Bride.

Our Lord: New Media is cold without your fire, noisy without your silence, and empty without your love. All technology is straw unless it draws us toward you. You have my thankfulness, my submission, and my heart — thank you for directing this story. May New Media both spread your grace and reveal the mystery of ages: that you are a bubbling Spring of Love.

Notes

Introduction // The Digital Continent

1. http://en.wikipedia.org/wiki/Fulton_J._Sheen#Radio.
2. http://en.wikipedia.org/wiki/Fulton_J._Sheen#Television.
3. http://en.wikipedia.org/wiki/Eternal_Word_Television_Network#Viewership_statistics.
4. http://idealsalesonline.com/webmasters/news_2010-03-11-06-58-51-188.html.
5. http://en.wikipedia.org/wiki/New_media.
6. http://www.mashable.com/2011/01/24/the-history-of-social-media-infographic.
7. http://blog.facebook.com/blog.php?post=72353897130.
8. https://sites.google.com/a/pressatgoogle.com/youtube5year/home/short-story-of-youtube.
9. http://en.wikipedia.org/wiki/Twitter.
10. http://www.onlineschools.org/blog/internet-stats.
11. http://www.huffingtonpost.com/2008/09/17/study-social-networking-s_n_127122.html.
12. http://techcrunch.com/2010/03/15/hitwise-says-facebook-most-popular-u-s-site.
13. http://www.techxav.com/2010/03/19/if-facebook-were-a-country.
14. http://www.facebook.com/press/info.php?statistics.
15. http://www.youtube.com/t/press_statistics.
16. http://www.twitaholic.com.
17. http://socialnomics.net/2009/08/11/statistics-show-social-media-is-bigger-than-you-think.
18. http://technorati.com/blogging/feature/state-of-the-blogosphere-2009.
19. http://www.edisonresearch.com/home/archives/2010/12/the_current_state_of_podcasting_2010.php.
20. http://pewInternet.org/Press-Releases/2010/Cell-phones-and-American-adults.aspx.
21. http://www.usatoday.com/yourlife/parenting-family/2010-12-30-1AYEAR30_CV_N.htm.
22. http://www.radiovaticana.org/EN1/Articolo.asp?c=374892.

Chapter 1 // The Virtual Areopagus: Digital Dialogue With the Unchurched

23. http://religions.pewforum.org/reports.
24. http://www.vatican.va/holy_father/john_paul_ii/messages/communications/documents/hf_jp-ii_mes_20020122_world-communications-day_en.html.
25. http://www.vatican.va/holy_father/benedict_xvi/messages/communications/documents/hf_ben-xvi_mes_20090124_43rd-world-communications-day_en.html.
26. Ibid.
27. http://blog.beliefnet.com/deaconsbench/2010/09/the-next-fulton-sheen.html.
28. http://www.vatican.va/archive/hist_councils/ii_vatican_council/documents/vat-ii_const_19651118_dei-verbum_en.html.

29. http://religions.pewforum.org/reports.
30. http://www.catholicscomehome.org/about-results-and-awards.php.
31. http://www.ewtnnews.com/catholic-news/new.php?id=2338.
32. http://catholicexchange.com/2010/12/03/142795.

Chapter 2 // Into the Light: Sharing the Spiritual Journey

33. http://www.vatican.va/roman_curia/pontifical_councils/pccs/documents/rc_pc_pccs_doc_23051971_communio_en.html.
34. http://www.convertjournal.com/p/convert-stories.html.
35. http://www.catholiceducation.org/articles/apologetics/ap0275.htm.

Chapter 3 // Speaking Their Language: Connecting With Young Adults

36. http://www.vatican.va/holy_father/benedict_xvi/messages/communications/documents/hf_ben-xvi_mes_20090124_43rd-world-communications-day_en.html.
37. *U.S. Religious Landscape Survey*, Pew Research Center's Forum on Religion & Public Life, September 2010.
38. *Sacraments Today: Belief and Practice Among U.S. Catholics*, Center for Applied Research in the Apostolate (CARA), February 2008.
39. Ibid.
40. Jessica E. Vascallero, "Why Email No Longer Rules: And what that means for the way we communicate," *Wall Street Journal* (October 12, 2009).
41. http://www.barna.org/barna-update/article/5-barna-update/127-twentysomethings-struggle-to-find-their-place-in-christian-churches.
42. http://www.pewInternet.org/Reports/2010/Social-Media-and-Young-Adults/Summary-of-Findings.aspx?r=1.
43. http://www.vatican.va/holy_father/john_paul_ii/encyclicals/documents/hf_jp-ii_enc_07121990_redemptoris-missio_en.html.
44. http://www.vatican.va/holy_father/benedict_xvi/messages/communications/documents/hf_ben-xvi_mes_20070124_41st-world-communications-day_en.html.

Chapter 4 // Modern Epistles: Blogging the Faith

45. Yes, this actually happened to a writer friend of mine.
46. http://www.vatican.va/roman_curia/pontifical_councils/pccs/documents/rc_pc_pccs_doc_23051971_communio_en.html.
47. http://www.usccb.org/meetings/2010Fall/2010-address-social-media.shtml.

Chapter 5 // New Wineskins: Fresh Presentations of Ancient Tradition

48. http://www.vatican.va/holy_father/john_paul_ii/messages/communications/documents/hf_jp-ii_mes_24011990_world-communications-day_en.html.
49. http://news.yahoo.com/s/nf/20110519/bs_nf/78635.

Chapter 6 // Digital Discourse: The New Apologetics

50. http://www.vatican.va/holy_father/john_paul_ii/messages/communications/documents/hf_jp-ii_mes_24011992_world-communications-day_en.html.

51. http://www.vatican.va/holy_father/john_paul_ii/apost_letters/documents/hf_jp-ii_apl_20010106_novo-millennio-ineunte_en.html.
52. http://www.facebook.com/pages/Patrick-Madrid/38585729301.
53. http://patrickmadrid.blogspot.com/2010/09/if-you-could-choose-theme-for-my-next.html.

Chapter 7 // Innovative Shepherding: New Media in the Diocese
54. http://www.vatican.va/roman_curia/pontifical_councils/pccs/documents/rc_pc_pccs_doc_22021992_aetatis_en.html.
55. http://www.usccb.org/comm/social-media-guidelines.shtml.
56. The USCCB's social-media guidelines (http://www.usccb.org/comm/social-media-guidelines.shtml) and the Children's Online Privacy Protection Act (http://www.ftc.gov/privacy/privacyinitiatives/childrens.html) are both available online.
57. http://www.vatican.va/roman_curia/pontifical_councils/new-evangelization/index.htm.

Chapter 8 // High-Tech Community: New Media in the Parish
58. http://www.catholicnewsagency.com/news/pope_benedict_to_promote_using_new_media_to_evangelize.
59. Ibid.
60. http://www.marketingpilgrim.com/2009/08/over-80-of-americans-use-social-media-monthly.html.
61. http://www.buzzplant.com/site/surveys/survey_results_church_sm.pdf.
62. http://www.vatican.va/holy_father/benedict_xvi/messages/communications/documents/hf_ben-xvi_mes_20100124_44th-world-communications-day_en.html.
63. http://www.textmessageblog.mobi/2010/08/10/text-messaging-use.
64. http://www.usccb.org/meetings/2010Fall/2010-address-social-media.shtml.
65. http://www.americancatholic.org/news/report.aspx?id=2682.

Chapter 9 // That They May Be One: Cultivating Online Community
66. http://www.vatican.va/holy_father/benedict_xvi/messages/communications/documents/hf_ben-xvi_mes_20090124_43rd-world-communications-day_en.html.
67. http://www.vatican.va/holy_father/john_paul_ii/messages/communications/documents/hf_jp-ii_mes_20020122_world-communications-day_en.html.
68. http://storico.radiovaticana.org/en3/storico/2009-12/346107_pope_benedict_s_general_prayer_intention_for_january_dedicated_to_young_people.html.
69. http://www.vatican.va/holy_father/benedict_xvi/messages/communications/documents/hf_ben-xvi_mes_20090124_43rd-world-communications-day_en.html.
70. http://www.vatican.va/holy_father/benedict_xvi/messages/communications/documents/hf_ben-xvi_mes_20110124_45th-world-communications-day_en.html.
71. Ibid.
72. http://twitter.com/search?q=%23cathmedia.

Chapter 10 // Changing the World: New Media Activism

73. http://www.firstthings.com/article/2008/04/europe-and-its-discontents---50.
74. http://www.vatican.va/holy_father/john_paul_ii/messages/communications/documents/hf_jp-ii_mes_20030124_world-communications-day_en.html.
75. http://www.vatican.va/holy_father/john_paul_ii/apost_letters/documents/hf_jp-ii_apl_20050124_il-rapido-sviluppo_en.html.
76. http://www.osjspm.org/catholic_social_teaching.aspx.
77. http://www.msnbc.msn.com/id/34850532/ns/technology_and_science-wireless.
78. http://www.vatican.va/holy_father/benedict_xvi/messages/communications/documents/hf_ben-xvi_mes_20110124_45th-world-communications-day_en.html.

Chapter 11 // Moving Mountains: Building a Digital Movement

79. http://www.vatican.va/holy_father/benedict_xvi/messages/communications/documents/hf_ben-xvi_mes_20060124_40th-world-communications-day_en.html.
80. http://www.vatican.va/holy_father/benedict_xvi/messages/communications/documents/hf_ben-xvi_mes_20090124_43rd-world-communications-day_en.html.
81. http://www.onlinemba.com/blog/the-stats-on-Internet-porn.
82. http://www.lightedcandle.org/pornstats/stats.asp.
83. http://pewsocialtrends.org/2010/11/18/the-decline-of-marriage-and-rise-of-new-families.
84. http://www.divorcerate.org.
85. http://en.wikipedia.org/wiki/Fulton_J._Sheen#Radio.

Conclusion // To Infinity and Beyond: The Future of the Church and New Media

86. http://www.nytimes.com/2010/11/30/opinion/30zhuo.html.
87. http://www.zenit.org/article-26438?l=english.
88. http://www.vatican.va/holy_father/john_paul_ii/messages/communications/documents/hf_jp-ii_mes_20020122_world-communications-day_en.html.
89. http://thenextweb.com/2009/09/15/ink-print-internet.
90. http://www.vatican.va/holy_father/john_paul_ii/messages/communications/documents/hf_jp-ii_mes_20020122_world-communications-day_en.html.
91. http://www.pewInternet.org/Reports/2011/Wikipedia.aspx.
92. Carr, Nicholas G. The Shallows: What the Internet Is Doing to Our Brains. New York: W.W. Norton, 2010.
93. Thanks to Father Robert Barron for that line.
94. http://www.trendsspotting.com/blog/?p=165.
95. http://www.dfwcatholic.org/vision-vocationmatchcom-results-of-annual-survey-on-trends-in-catholic-religious-vocations-3203/.html.
96. http://www.bridgeportdiocese.com/index.php/fcc/article/2011_0516tweet.
97. http://www.time.com/time/specials/packages/article/0,28804,2036683_2037183,00.html.

98. http://fourstory.org/features/story/social-media-and-social-justice-facebook-causes.

99. http://www.vatican.va/holy_father/john_paul_ii/apost_letters/documents/hf_jp-ii_apl_20050124_il-rapido-sviluppo_en.html.

Afterword

100. *Compendium of the Social Doctrine of the Church*, n. 414 (http://www.vatican.va/roman_curia/pontifical_councils/justpeace/documents/rc_pc_justpeace_doc_20060526_compendio-dott-soc_en.html).

101. http://www.vatican.va/holy_father/benedict_xvi/messages/communications/documents/hf_ben-xvi_mes_20110124_45th-world-communications-day_en.html.

102. Pope Pius XI, encyclical letter *Divini Illius Magistri* (December 31, 1929), nn. 89-91 (http://www.vatican.va/holy_father/pius_xi/encyclicals/documents/hf_p-xi_enc_31121929_divini-illius-magistri_en.html).

103. Pope Pius XI, encyclical letter *Vigilanti Cura* (June 29, 1936) (http://www.vatican.va/holy_father/pius_xi/encyclicals/documents/hf_p-xi_enc_29061936_vigilanti-cura_en.html); Pope Pius XII, encyclical letter *Miranda Prorsus* (September 8, 1957) (http://www.vatican.va/holy_father/pius_xii/encyclicals/documents/hf_p-xii_enc_08091957_miranda-prorsus_en.html); Second Vatican Council, conciliar decree *Inter Mirifica* (December 4, 1963) (http://www.vatican.va/archive/hist_councils/ii_vatican_council/documents/vat-ii_decree_19631204_inter-mirifica_en.html); Pontifical Commission for Social Communications, pastoral instruction *Communio et Progressio* (May 23, 1971) (http://www.vatican.va/roman_curia/pontifical_councils/pccs/documents/rc_pc_pccs_doc_23051971_communio_en.html); Pontifical Council for Social Communications, pastoral instruction *Aetatis Novae* (February 22, 1992) (http://www.vatican.va/roman_curia/pontifical_councils/pccs/documents/rc_pc_pccs_doc_22021992_aetatis_en.html). The 45 papal messages for World Communications Day have been delivered by Popes Paul VI (1-12), John Paul II (13-39), and Benedict XVI (40-45).

104. Pontifical Commission for Social Communications, pastoral instruction *Communio et Progressio* (May 23, 1971), n. 106 (http://www.vatican.va/roman_curia/pontifical_councils/pccs/documents/rc_pc_pccs_doc_23051971_communio_en.html).

105. For this quote, see http://www.vatican.va/roman_curia/pontifical_councils/pccs/documents/rc_pc_pccs_doc_19031986_guide-for-future-priests_en.html.

106. Second Vatican Council, decree *Christus Dominus* (October 28, 1965), n. 13. For this quote, see link in ibid.

Book Royalties and Computer Project

107. http://www.vatican.va/holy_father/benedict_xvi/messages/communications/documents/hf_ben-xvi_mes_20090124_43rd-world-communications-day_en.html.

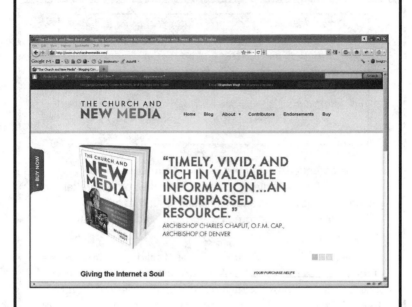

Intrigued by what you read in this book?

Want to learn more about the Church and technology?

Looking for additional New Media resources, advice, or tips?

Head over to **www.ChurchAndNewMedia.com** for even more material, including:

- A blog featuring relevant articles, tech-tips, and links to other Catholic New Media content.

- A resources page linking to content mentioned in the book as well as many additional items.

- More information about each of the book's contributors.

BOOK ROYALTIES AND COMPUTER PROJECT

> *"It would be a tragedy for the future of humanity if the new instruments of communication ... should contribute only to increasing the gap separating the poor from the new networks that are developing at the service of human socialization and information."*[107]
>
> — POPE BENEDICT XVI, MESSAGE FOR THE 43RD WORLD COMMUNICATIONS DAY (2009)

One potential effect of the New Media revolution is a deepening of the so-called digital divide. As the computer-literacy gap between developed and developing countries widens, those without online access become further separated both socially and economically.

Practicing the Catholic social theme of solidarity, **100 percent of the royalties from this book are going toward establishing school computer labs throughout the Archdiocese of Mombasa, Kenya.** Besides providing the computer hardware and software for children in poor, rural areas, the kids will be trained in computer-literacy skills. For scores of children, this book will be a ticket to the "digital continent."

You can make an additional donation to the project online through the **Church and New Media** website (www.ChurchAndNewMedia.com) or through **Catholic Relief Services** (http://Donate.CRS.org/ComputersKenya). Alternatively, you can donate by sending a check to the Catholic Relief Services address below with "Computers for Kids in Kenya" on the check's memo line:

CATHOLIC RELIEF SERVICES
P.O. BOX 17090
BALTIMORE, MD 21203-7090

Please note: Contributions to CRS will be used for the purpose(s), if any, specified by the donor. However, if in the judgment of CRS, such purpose(s) become unnecessary, undesirable, impractical, or impossible to fulfill, CRS may use such contributions for its general charitable purposes.